A GRIM ALMANAC OF

LINCOLNSHIRE

For Julia and Nigel

A Grim Almanac of

LINCOLNSHIRE

Neil R. Storey

Officers and men from the Holland and Kesteven subdivisions of Lincolnshire Constabulary at Spalding, *c.* 1912.

Frontispiece: Lincoln city and cathedral, viewed from Canwick Road Cemetery.

First published 2011

The History Press
The Mill, Brimscombe Port
Stroud, Gloucestershire, GL5 2QG
www.thehistorypress.co.uk

British Library Cataloguing in Publication Data.
A catalogue record for this book is available from the British Library.

ISBN 978 0 7524 5768 0

Typesetting and origination by The History Press
Printed in Malta by Melita Press

CONTENTS

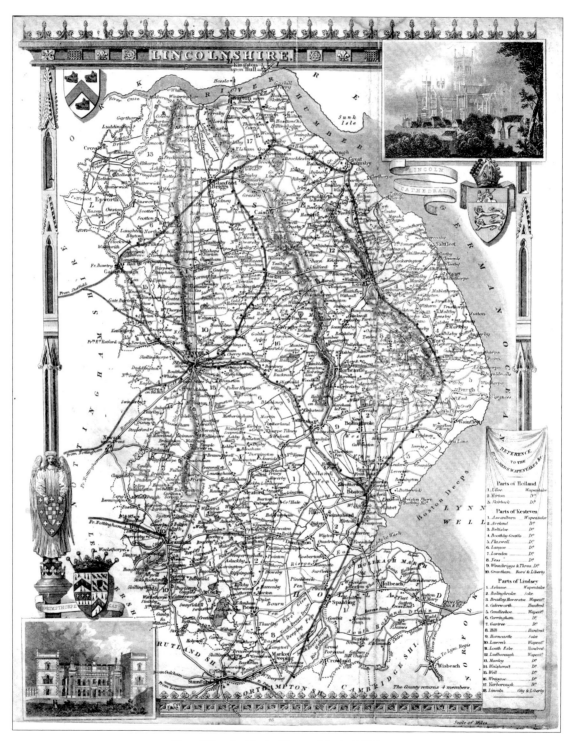

Map of Lincolnshire by Thomas Moule, 1838.

ACKNOWLEDGEMENTS

Writing this book has proved to me, yet again, that you meet some of the nicest people when researching the grimmest tales. There really are too many individuals to mention them all by name but I wish to record particular thanks to the following, without whom this book would not have been so enriched: first and foremost, my friend and fellow crime historian Stewart P. Evans and his good lady, Rosie; Lincolnshire County Council; Lincolnshire Local Studies Library at the Lincoln Central Library; Lincoln Castle Museum; North Lincolnshire Reference Library; Lincoln Cathedral; the Church of St Lawrence and St George, Springthorpe; the Museum of Lincolnshire Life, Lincoln; Lincoln Tourist Information Centre; Alan Tutt, Stamford Museum; the George Hotel, Stamford; Robert Pacy, Old Chapel Lane Books, Burgh le Marsh; St Marys Books and Prints, Stamford; St Paul's Street Bookshop, Stamford; Robert Bell at Wisbech & Fenland Museum; Crowland Abbey; University of East Anglia Library; Robert 'Bookman' Wright; Elaine Abel; Margaret Whitby-Green, the creator of the Original Lincolnshire Ghost Walk; Matilda Richards and Jenny Briancourt at The History Press; and, last but by no means least, I thank my darling Molly and son Lawrence for their love, and their interest in my research for this book.

All images are from the author's archive unless otherwise stated. Every effort has been made to obtain permission from copyright holders; any omission is unintentional and no offence was intended. All modern images were taken by the author at locations across Lincolnshire between 2009 and 2011.

INTRODUCTION

Truth is always strange;
Stranger than fiction

Lord Byron, *Don Juan* (1823)

I have travelled most of eastern England in search of the strange, folkloric, ghostly and the macabre, but have enjoyed a warm welcome wherever I have visited. However, there is something special about the warmth and kindness of Lincolnshire people that particularly stands out, and I shall look forward to future excursions across fen and wold in that remarkable county. That said, when one gazes across the Fenland in winter – with your back to the wind and drizzle, feeling the cold bite into the back of the neck whilst you peer across those miles of flat wetland, picking out the spires of the churches and landmarks from the gloomy, grey mist as the late afternoon light fades – one's mind can soon wander to the darker history of the place. For this land has seen crimes, dark deeds and misfortunes provoked by loneliness, hunger, depravations and desperation.

It certainly did not take much for me to envisage the Tiddy Mun lurking around the waters, to imagine the Black Dog loping along a lonely track, or even a hytersprite appearing to lead me to my doom in those murky, cold, water channels. Like most of East Anglia, an ardent belief in folklore and witchcraft was once widespread in Lincolnshire, and lingered far longer than in many other parts of our country; for some it is still very much alive today.

The ancient Fen folk themselves are a lost breed; they were formidable and, to the outsiders whom they did not welcome or trust, they seemed a race apart. Perhaps that is why St Guthlac, the founder of Crowland Abbey, lived in a wattle hut on an island when he first fled to the Fens in the eighth century. He was troubled there by what he described as 'develen and luther gostes', who tugged him and led him out of his cot to the fen, where they threw and sunk him in the muddy waters, then beat him with iron whips. In his *Britannia* (1586), William Camden described these creatures as:

...the divels of Crowland, with their blabber lips, fire-spitting mouths, rough and skaly visages, beetle heads, terrible teeth, sharpe chins, hoarse throats, blacke skinns, crump-shoulders, side and gorbellies, burning loines, crooked and hawm'd legs, long tailed buttocks, and ugly mishapes, which heeretofore walked and wandered up and downe in these places, and very much troubled holy Guthlake and the Monkes.

Today, visitors flock to the seaside resorts to the east of the Lincolnshire Wolds, but, not that long ago, before the tourist trade took off, the Lincolnshire coastline was the haunt of smugglers, known locally as 'owlers'. Their trade extended back centuries, but was particularly prevalent in the eighteenth and nineteenth centuries when they ran cargos of tobacco, tea, sugar and Dutch gin by the cartload, from the coast to the county, during the dead of night. The excise men – be they riding officers, foot patrols, or aboard their sloops, patrolling along the coast and The Wash – had their work cut out for them, with such places as Skegness and Mablethorpe becoming infamous hotbeds of formidable smuggler gangs. Villagers further inland, notably those living around Louth and Horncastle, also became adept at maintaining hiding places, refuges and 'runs' for smugglers. It is even said that Dent's Creek, on the Humber, saw so many Dutchmen passing through that locals called the area Little Holland. To enable such a trade to thrive, it was essential that all those involved knew how to keep their mouths shut; there was always the fear of reprisals from the gangs if someone did give up a smuggler to the law, but it seems that most folks enjoyed a little tipple or a smoke courtesy of the 'owlers' and were happy to 'Watch the wall, my darling, while the Gentlemen go by!' That is not to say that there were no vicious exchanges between the excise men and the owlers. One story tells of how a 'Duty Man' came off worse from one such fight, died from his wounds, and was buried in the wall of the Vine Inn at Skegness. His body was only uncovered during building renovations in 1902; the fragments of his uniform and buttons, which carried the royal crest, were the only clues to his identity.

Even the woods, forests and country estates of Lincolnshire have their fair share of crime. During the nineteenth century, poaching was rife across the county and the crimes of theft, trespass and, above all, offences against the Game Laws, absorbed the majority of the magistrates' time; it is hardly surprising that the best-known folk song of the county is 'The Lincolnshire Poacher'. The open highway was not much better, as the roads of Lincolnshire were frequently the haunt of highway robbers, including the notorious Dick Turpin.

Francis Dashwood, 15th Baron le Despencer, was so concerned for the safety of travellers on the Lincolnshire roads that he built a 'land lighthouse' (now known as Dunston Pillar) high above his estate, to shine a powerful light across the countryside to deter the highwaymen who lurked in the darkness. Dashwood, however, had his own dark secret, for it was he who founded the Hell Fire Club. The stories of what occurred at the secret meetings of this elite fraternity were legendary, and their behaviour was said to be so outrageous and debauched that Dashwood and the other members of the club were widely believed to be involved in Devil worship. Whether this was true or not, I am sure that Dashwood enjoyed the notoriety brought about by such rumours.

Even in long-established urban areas there are tales to be found, both criminal and folkloric. One man who stands out on our grim tour is William Marwood, a Horncastle cobbler. This quiet, staunch Methodist was our nation's executioner from 1874 until his death in 1883. Marwood was responsible for introducing the 'Long Drop' to British executions, whereby the condemned would suffer a calculated drop,

The Lincoln Imp.

resulting in their neck being broken, instead of the prolonged strangling that had been the hallmark of executions for centuries before. A total of 176 condemned felons kept an appointment with Mr Marwood – the scientific hangman.

Lincoln Guildhall and Stonebow on Saltergate, *c.* 1905. The city gaol was located in the Guildhall for many years, with a dungeon for felons and a small debtors' prison at street level.

Another infamous Lincolnshire character – whose visage is far better known, having appeared on everything from toasting forks to souvenir china – is a 12in-stone carving dating from the thirteenth century, known to all as the Lincoln Imp. The ancient legend tells how the imp was sent by the Devil and was carried on the winds to the cathedral, where he tried to trip up the Lord Bishop, knock down the Dean and goad the vergers and choir. When he started to break the windows the angels told him to desist, but the imp replied, 'Stop me if you can!' Whereupon he was instantly turned to stone and will sit for evermore, high in a cleft above the north side of the Angel Choir.

In a county so rich in history and legend, it is not surprising that Lincolnshire has numerous literary connections, among them no lesser luminaries than Sir Walter Scott (who would often stop off at the George Hotel in Stamford as he travelled down the Great North Road to London from his Scottish home) and of course Alfred, Lord Tennyson, a true son of the county, born at Somersby. Perhaps they drew inspiration for some of their works as they passed through the county. Great composers such as Vaughan Williams and Percy Grainger most certainly visited the county, and drew upon the traditional music of rural Lincolnshire – for here was to be found a host of native people, places and events with the colour and character to be a wealth of inspiration. The county was also fortunate to have its folklore, customs and stories loyally collected and recorded, by individuals such as Ethel Rudkin, Henry Winn, Robert Heanley and Christopher Marlowe – without whom, much of the local lore and beliefs of the county would have been lost for future generations. Other stories have remained buried for years in cuttings books, old newspapers, antiquarian manuscripts, and assize and sessions records – until now. The dust has been blown off a number of long-stored boxes, and the pages turned on old books and papers; many of these forgotten stories are recounted within this volume.

This book is a journey through some of the darkest moments of Lincolnshire's past, a truly grim assemblage of miscreants, murderers and misdeeds – some well known and some obscure. This diverse collection ranges from the Bottesford privy tragedy and the Heckington hypochondriac, to the Wrangle poisoner and the 'Acid Bath Murderer'. Upon these pages is recorded a cornucopia of the strange, unfortunate, tragic and the macabre; a grim tale for every day of the year. So, if you have the curiosity to look through a dark mirror into the sinister past of Lincolnshire, and the stomach for it, read on gentle reader ... if you dare.

Neil R. Storey, 2011

JANUARY

Wainfleet High Street, *c.* 1900.

The Wainfleet Riot, January 1833

About 300 Fen embankers or 'navvies' were employed upon the new navigation near Burgh; these men were far from popular among the indigenous Fen folk, as the *Lincolnshire Chronicle* reported: 'About 70 of these semi-savages arrived at Wainfleet where they remained "randying" as they term drinking, making no secret of their intention. They were joined in the afternoon by about 30 or more.'

They began by driving all the market people and others out of the Angel Inn, using the most horrid language and threatening to murder any who opposed them. Mr Maulkinson, the landlord, was knocked down and seriously injured by one of them. The rioters then rushed out into the street, cheering, holding up their tools, and attacking the shops. Local constables, aided by the principal inhabitants, used forks and other weapons that they could procure to drive rioters from the town.

1 JANUARY **1886** Frederick Overton, a helper at the stud of Lord Yarborough, was taken to task about drinking too much beer by John Cheales, his lordship's groom. Overton replied, 'I'm ready to go if anyone can be found to do my work better!' Cheales's response was to give Overton a week's notice to quit. Overton spat back, 'If you discharge me you are a dead man,' and marched off. At 9 p.m. Overton went to the gun room and helped himself to a revolver and five cartridges, saying he wanted to use them on a troublesome cat. He proceeded to the house of John Cheales, to have the matter out. An argument ensued and Overton drew the weapon; immediately, Mrs Cheales pushed Overton and the gun went off – the bullet narrowly missed John Cheales's head but a second shot scorched his shirt sleeve. Overton tried to fire once more but the weapon failed to discharge. Arrested and brought before the Lincoln Assizes, Overton claimed that he had acted under the influence of drink and could not be held fully responsible for his actions. Found guilty of shooting with intent to murder, Overton was sentenced to thirty years' penal servitude.

2 JANUARY **1900** John Jubb (65), a platelayer who had been employed for many years on the Great Central Railway, was walking over the Trent railway bridge at Bole for the purpose of fog signalling. Hearing a train coming, he stepped onto the other set of rails and was instantly knocked down and killed by the 11.37 'Great Eastern Express' from Doncaster. Unfortunately, two trains had come at the same time; the fog had been so dense that neither engine driver could see any distance ahead, and poor John Jubb didn't have a hope.

3 JANUARY **1900** Matthew Depear (77) burnt to death at his home in Whaplode Fen near Spalding. Alone in the house, he appeared to have fallen onto the fire and was unable to extricate himself. This was the sixth tragic death reported to the Spalding coroner within a week of Christmas.

4 JANUARY **1928** Bertram Kirby was hanged at HMP Lincoln by Thomas Pierrepoint. Bert and Minnie Kirby had seemed to live quietly at their bungalow in Louth. In July 1927, Bert's business had failed and he was in financial trouble. Suddenly, he had gone around claiming that he and his wife had sold the bungalow and were going to be away for a while. One of their grown-up sons became concerned when he called round and found he was locked out of the house. Police were called and forced entry – inside they found the body of Minnie Kirby, battered to death with an axe. A police search was mounted for Bert; when he was tracked down, and told that he was wanted for questioning with regard to his wife's death, he replied, 'All right, I'm not going to cause you any trouble. By God boy, you don't know what things are. I hope you never will. You don't know what I've had to put up with.' Kirby pleaded insanity at his

The tragic end of
Matthew Depear.

trial and even tried to commit suicide twice but, found guilty of murder,
he kept his appointment with the executioner on this day.

1860 In a report of abandoned vessels, it was noted that a billyboy **5 JANUARY**
schooner named *Rover*, of Goole, was brought into Grimsby. When the
vessel was discovered, there was a fire in the cabin and a lamp burning –
but not a soul was found on board. A few days later, another vessel, the
brig *Favourite*, of London, was found drifting and was towed to Grimsby.
This time life was found aboard – a little boy, nearly dead for want of food.

1893 John Presgrave (15) had been visiting his grandmother in Boston **6 JANUARY**
and was skating back along the Forty Foot Drain to the farm where he
was employed at Quadring. As he sped under a bridge, the ice gave way;
the poor boy fell in and drowned. The inquest jury recommended that
notices should be posted at all bridges when the ice was not safe.

1865 The arsonists responsible for the recent fire at the stack yard of **7 JANUARY**
Farmer Johnson, near the centre of the village of Appleby, were reportedly
captured. The stacks would have been consumed by the flames had it not
been for the fact that neighbours and local farmers had invested in a new
fire engine, which was put into action for the first time at this incident. The
Winterton fire engine also attended, but nevertheless two straw stacks,
an oat stack and a wheat stack were lost, and a large stack of beans was
partly destroyed. The smoke from the fire could be seen for some miles
around and caused concern in the surrounding villages, especially Brigg.

The men apprehended by Superintendent Aslin for starting the fire were both farm workers.

8 JANUARY **Strange Tales and Folklore of Lincolnshire: Plough Monday – be generous or beware!** Plough Monday was usually celebrated on the first Monday after Twelfth Night or Epiphany. It was the day when ploughs were blessed in special church services, and the first furrow was cut on the land to mark the start of the new farming year; there were also some rural festivities to be had. One Plough Monday in Lincolnshire was recorded by someone who observed it first-hand during the mid-nineteenth century. The following was published in the *Book of Days* in 1864:

> Rude though it was, the Plough procession threw a life into the dreary scenery of winter ... It was nothing unusual for at least a score of the 'sons of the soil' to yoke themselves as Plough Bullocks with ropes to the plough having put on clean smock-frocks in honour of the day. There was no limit to the number who joined in the Morris-dance and were partners with 'Bessy' who carried the money box and all these had ribbons in their hats and pinned about them wherever there was room to display a bunch ... Some wore small bunches of corn in their hats, from which the wheat was soon shaken out by the ungainly jumping which they called dancing. Occasionally, if the winter was severe, the procession was joined by threshers carrying their flails, reapers bearing their sickles and carters with their long whips which they were ever cracking to add to the noise, while even the smith and the miller were among the number and Bessy rattled his box and danced so

The 'Procession of the Plough' during the celebrations on Plough Monday.

high that he shewed his worsted stockings and corduroy breeches. For Bessy is to the procession of Plough Monday jest that would call up the angry blush to a modest cheek. Reciting their verses and 'God Speed the Plough' even the poorest cottagers dropped a few pence into Bessy's box or gave a gift of bread or ale. At the large farm house, besides money they obtained their food and ale for the day and their 'load' of similar for their celebrations by night.

But the great event of the day was when they came before some house which bore signs that the owner was well-to-do in the world and nothing was given to them. Bessy rattled his box and the ploughmen danced, while the country lads blew their bullocks' horns or shouted with all their might but if there was still no sign, no coming forth of bread and cheese or ale, then the word was given, the ploughshare driven into the ground before the door or window, the whole twenty men yoked pulling like one and in a minute or two the ground before the house was as brown, barren and ridgy as a newly-ploughed field.

9 JANUARY

1885 Findings were published from the inquest on the death of Lemuel Simpson Pepperdine. Pepperdine was the young manager of a branch of Harston's chemist in Lincoln. He had visited a neighbouring village on a Sunday and had not returned home until Tuesday evening. On his return, he had complained of being tired and went to his bedroom with a bottle of prussic acid to rub on his leg, which he claimed was causing him pain. Later that evening, his door was found to be locked and, after an entry was forced, he was discovered insensible in bed, having drunk the contents of the prussic acid bottle and another of laudanum. He died before the doctor arrived. Death was recorded as being by his own hand but a motive was not recorded.

10 JANUARY

1868 Lincolnshire Quarter Sessions reports were published, detailing the conviction of a railway policeman, Stephen Sage (40), and pointsman and watchman George Turner (39), for felony. Their haul consisted of two geese and five ducks. The birds had gone missing from the Yarborough Arms and Railway Hotel, New Holland. County police had traced footprints to a hut on the railway where Turner was working, and some down was found sticking to his jacket. His boots matched the tracks from the crime scene perfectly. His house was searched and the birds were soon discovered. Upon his arrest, Turner implicated Sage and gave evidence against him, perhaps in the hope of reducing his own sentence. Both were found guilty and sentenced to six months' imprisonment with hard labour.

11 JANUARY

1904 A tramp, who gave his name as Fisher, was searched on admission to Lincoln Prison. The searching warder found a pocketbook and saw the innocuous name of a flower, 'Narcissus'. The warder was a keen gardener and asked the prisoner if he shared the same interest, whereupon the latter snatched a leaf from the book and thrust it in his mouth. The paper was only extracted after some struggle; the chewed page then revealed references to a Kidderminster murder and words to the effect 'I murdered her. God help me. Murder will out.' Suspicions were communicated with Worcestershire Police, who identified Fisher as the last man seen in the company of a woman hop-picker who had been brutally murdered.

12 JANUARY **1889** On this day, a Saturday afternoon football match ended in tragedy. Staveley Football Club was playing against Grimsby Town FC at Clee Park, Grimsby when, a quarter of an hour into the game, a collision occurred. Daniel Doyle, one of Grimsby's fullbacks, breasted the ball in an attempt to get it from William Cropper (a distinguished Derbyshire Cricketer), one of the Staveley forwards. As he jumped, Doyle struck Cropper in the stomach with his knee. Cropper fell down and had to be led off the field but was not thought to be seriously injured – although, he did say as he left, 'They have killed me.' Cropper was keen to point out that he blamed no one, but his condition rapidly deteriorated. He did not leave the dressing room and died there the following morning. The inquest returned a verdict of 'accidental death'.

13 JANUARY **1881** Elizabeth Brown, housekeeper to Mr Bennett at Kirmington, had not been herself for some time – to the degree that Bennett felt it necessary to discharge her, upon which she threw herself into the pond. Before this incident, friends had been so concerned about her that they had tried to place her in an asylum, but had failed to obtain the requisite medical certificate. On this day, the Bench sentenced her to be detained in Her Majesty's Prison at Lincoln for six weeks and instructed the Governor, Major Mackay, to report her case to the Visiting Justices at the termination of her sentence.

14 JANUARY **1882** Dr Mitcheson held an inquest at Gainsborough upon the body of Mr Thomas Oldman, the solicitor and coroner for North Lincolnshire. Mr Oldman had attended to his professional duties during the day but had then gone home and dropped dead in his own dining room. The jury returned a verdict of 'death from a rupture of a blood vessel on the brain'.

15 JANUARY **1867** A Gainsborough coroner's inquest recorded the body of Eliza Hannah Glover (3) as 'found dead'. Eliza had been the illegitimate child of Sarah Blow from before her marriage to Alfred Blow, who worked at the tan yard of Mr Hiley. It was clear that Eliza had not been wanted – she had been found in a filthy state with numerous cuts and injuries upon her tiny body. Mr and Mrs Blow claimed that Eliza was in a bad state because she had recently recovered from a bout of measles, and that her injuries had been sustained from a fall down the stairs. The police pressed for a post-mortem, which was conducted by Dr Duigan; among his horrible catalogue of findings were open wounds on Eliza's loins (caused from

The shocking discovery of the unwanted, wasted and beaten child.

being tied into a chair on a regular basis) and, most heartrending of all, she had been deprived of food (she weighed just 13½lbs). No trace of food was found inside her and her impending death from starvation had been hastened by wounds inflicted upon her head. Sarah and Alfred Blow were brought before the Lincoln Assizes. Witnesses stated that they had seen Mr Blow hit the child on the head with a cane, knock the child down with his hand and, on one occasion, had put her up a chimney while the fire was burning. Sarah Blow was no better; she had been heard to urge on her husband's maltreatment, with cries of 'Hit it, hit it!' She was also heard to declare to others about her child, 'I wish it were dead,' and 'If I can get shut of the child, my husband will behave better to me.' Both Sarah and Alfred Blow were found guilty of manslaughter and were each sentenced to fifteen years' penal servitude.

16 JANUARY

1880 Michael Cosgrove (42) and Bridget Cosgrove (32) were brought before Lincolnshire Epiphany Sessions charged with assaulting Catherine McGrath, causing her grievous bodily harm in Wroot. All three had been members of a potato picking party, living in a barn while they worked. Bridget had called Catherine a foul name and struck her twice with a stick. Mr Cosgrove had then struck Catherine to the ground; she got up, only to be knocked down again by Mr Cosgrove, who then kicked her and jumped on her. Other people in the barn could not interfere – Bridget held a knife in her hand and threatened to run it through their hearts if they tried. The Cosgroves finished their violence and walked away. Dr Cameron was called from Epworth and the constable was soon on the scene too. After a week in a critical condition, Catherine McGrath began her recovery. When brought before the court, the Cosgroves gave no reason for the attack. Found guilty, Bridget Cosgrove was sentenced to one year's hard labour. Michael Cosgrove had already served ten years' penal servitude for another offence and was sentenced to five years' hard labour.

17 JANUARY   **Cures of Cunning Folk in Fen and Wold: The Wonders of Dung**
Early morning dew on a cowpat was seen as a particularly efficacious cure for spots and blemishes. If you put your finger in the moisture, and dabbed it on your acne spot or 'push', the flaw was said to soon clear up. The healing powers of dung dew were also said to have remarkable qualities – take one spoon of it a day and you would be cured of tuberculosis.

If you were suffering from chilblains, a cure oft suggested well into the twentieth century was to hop out into the field, find a nice fresh cowpat, and put your foot in it.

Dung, and the 'healing herbs within it', when mingled with honey and warmed over a slow fire then applied as a poultice, was also said to cure persistent boils and breast abscesses. Startling a cow and making it drop its dung was said to make a fine poultice to blanch freckles and the marks of ringworm. A dung poultice was even used as a cure for babies' cradle cap. Chicken or goose dung, regularly massaged into the scalp, was considered an effective cure for baldness.

18 JANUARY   **1850**   A Louth inquest published its findings on the body of Joseph Leaf, bricklayer and beerhouse keeper of Northgate. It appeared that Leaf had, in recent years, developed drunken habits, and 'was frequently partially deranged in mind in consequence'. He had left his companions at a beerhouse, saying, 'I hope I'll meet you in Heaven.' He was found the following morning drowned in a water tank, with one arm and one leg tied together with his handkerchief. A verdict of 'suicide during a fit of temporary insanity' was recorded.

19 JANUARY   **1892**   Ben Dickinson (32), an employee of Gibson's Coal Merchants, was affixing labels to a coal truck on the Great Northern Railway siding at Sleaford. Rather than going around a nearby goods truck, he attempted to cross the line underneath it. However, the goods train began to shunt, causing the wheels of the truck to pass over both of Dickinson's legs. Dr Jacobson was summoned to the scene and Dickinson was conveyed to Boston Hospital by special train. Upon arrival there, Dr Pilcher of the medical staff examined the wounds, and found that not only were the patient's legs crushed but there were also massive internal injuries. Poor Ben Dickinson died two hours later.

1858   The case of Thomas Boules (69) was reported. Described in court
as an 'incorrigible plunderer', Boules was utterly destitute yet would not
stay put in the workhouse. At the Louth Sessions, he was charged by
PC Bell with being found upon the premises of Mr William East, of
Maiden Row, for unlawful purposes at 3 a.m. Boules admitted that he
had been stealing fuel, and PC Bell pointed out that he had driven Boules
away from the coal and timber yard on a number of previous occasions.
It was also remarked that Boules had recently been released from prison
for a similar offence. The magistrate ordered that Boules be taken to
the workhouse and, if found in similar circumstances again, was to be
committed for trial.

1882   Reports were published of the district coroner's inquest on the
body of publican, William Barton (56). The deceased man had sent for his
doctor, who found him suffering from the effects of drink and prescribed
him an opiate. The following day, Barton was spotted walking quickly
from his garden to the countryside; in fact, he walked 2 miles to Louth
Canal, where he threw himself in. When his body was recovered, all life
was extinct. The inquest returned a verdict of 'temporary insanity'.

1858   Reports were published on the case of Mary Ann Hammond (7),
who was brought before the Sessions at Louth. Mary was the daughter
of William and Elizabeth Hammond of Spital Hill – a notorious vagrant
couple and bad characters, who often sent their children out to beg and
steal. Poor little Mary had been caught in the shop of Mr Johnson the
confectioner, in Eastgate, while attempting to steal money from the till.
She was so diminutive that she had crept around the counter unseen by
Mr Johnson, but had been spotted in the act by a customer. The police were
called and the girl was searched. A pair of jet bracelets were found in her
possession; she had stolen these from Mr Wilman, the Eastgate toy dealer.
The mother of the child admitted that she had sent Mary out to beg.

   As the evidence of a child so young could not be received, nor could she
be committed to prison, the magistrate adjourned the case to consider
what course he could pursue with respect to the parents.

1858   William Banks kept a common tramp lodging house in
Walkergate, Louth. He was also a hawker of cockles (hence his nickname
'Cockle Billy') and always took his formidable dog along with him. John
Hewson, a druggist in Mercer Row, was passing along the street when
the dog ran out from under the cart and went for him, biting him on
the thigh. Hewson complained that the dog should have been muzzled
but, upon hearing that the dog had bitten other people, he requested that
Banks destroy the animal. Banks initially refused, but, with his court
appearance imminent, he did so, and the court allowed the withdrawal
of the complaint on payment of *7s 6d*.

24 JANUARY   **1817**   A shocking occurrence in the parish workhouse at Whaplode, near Spalding, was reported. John Paling, a pauper, was in the back kitchen when he complained of being ill. Elizabeth Hardy, a woman in her early 20s, who had become blind after contracting smallpox at the age of 10 and had been an inmate of the workhouse ever since, went to see what was wrong. It appeared that Paling had been feigning sickness, using this as a ruse to get Elizabeth into the kitchen. Paling began to laugh and play with her, but after about ten minutes of this behaviour he suddenly stabbed Elizabeth in the throat; she staggered into another room and died. A coroner's inquest was held on the body, and a verdict of 'wilful murder' was recorded against Paling. The coroner committed him to Lincoln Assizes. When brought up, Paling stared wildly about the court and witnesses proved that he had suffered bouts of mental instability. The jury found him not guilty, on the grounds of insanity.

Broadside illustration of John Paling stabbing Elizabeth Hardy.

25 JANUARY   **Cures of Cunning Folk in Fen and Wold: Hedgehogs**
Cures obtained from gypsies were considered particularly potent; a number of these were based around hedgehogs. Gypsies ate hedgehogs after baking them in mud casings – when the mud was peeled away the spines went with it, leaving the cooked meat. New mothers were often prescribed this food, as it was believed that it enriched their blood after childbirth; the same food was offered as a treatment for those suffering with anaemia.

Mother hedgehog
and her young – an
old Lincolnshire
cure.

Punishments of the Past: The Stocks

The parish stocks were the oldest and most widely used punitive device for minor offenders, such as beggars, drunkards, louts, prostitutes and scolds. In the close-knit communities of the past, retribution against those who transgressed the social or moral codes was both public and humiliating. The stocks consisted of two sturdy uprights fixed in the ground, with grooves in their inner surfaces in which were slotted two solid timber boards, one above the other. Each plank had semi-circles cut in it which, when aligned together, formed holes which encircled the culprit's ankles. With the upper plank held in position by a padlock, there was no escape for the victim until he or she was released by the parish constable, beadle or similar appointed official. The authorities considered it so important for villages to have stocks that Acts decreeing this were passed in the fourteenth and fifteenth centuries. The absence of stocks and a whipping post in a village, after 1405, would downgrade the status of a village to a mere hamlet. Utilised heavily in the eighteenth century, stocks were known to be used for drunken miscreants up to the late nineteenth century. Good examples of stocks can still be found in the county at Pinchbeck, Alford, and Witham on the Hill; a fine reproduction set, built on the site of the originals, can be seen in Alvingham.

1961   The last execution at HMP Lincoln was carried out on this day by Harry Allen, upon Wasyl Gnypiuk. Gnypiuk (34) was a Polish-Ukrainian immigrant who had murdered widow Louisa Surgey (64) at Worksop on 17 July 1960. The two had become acquainted when Gnypiuk first rented

Alvingham stocks and whipping post.

a room from Louisa. On the night in question, Gnypiuk was destitute and had returned to Mrs Surgey's house to see if she would allow him to stay. Gaining entry, he found a bottle of spirits in the kitchen and went into the lounge, lay down on the settee and started drinking. Mrs Surgey's decapitated body was found on an allotment the following morning. Her head was found about a mile away in a carrier bag. Gnypiuk claimed that he had been drunk and in a deep sleep, and had dreamt that he was strangling Louisa. When he awoke, he had discovered the dead body and panicked. Tried at the Nottinghamshire Assizes, Gnypiuk's story failed to convince the jury – especially when it was found that he had taken £250 from Mrs Surgey, an ideal amount to pay off some of his debts. Found guilty of the murder, he was sent to the gallows.

28 JANUARY **1790**   Newspapers reported a boxing match at Waddington, near Lincoln, between two women from the village, Susanna Locker and Mary Farmery. Both had laid claim to the affections of the same young man, out of which arose a challenge from the latter woman to fight for the prize – which was accepted. Proper sidesmen were chosen and every matter was conducted in form. After several blows on each side, the battle ended in favour of Mary Farmery.

29 JANUARY **1893**   The body of an old soldier named Bedford (60) was discovered by local carrier Joseph Green, on a footpath between Branston Fen and Washingborough. Bedford had been residing for some time at the Green Tree Inn near the fen, and had earned a little money working with threshing machines in the neighbourhood. The day before his body was found, he had called in at the Royal Oak Inn at Washingborough, where he had asked for two-penny's worth of whisky and hot water, saying that he was ill. He left shortly after and was walked part of the way home by a Mr Johnson. Bedford was spotted lying on the floor, apparently asleep, at about 6 o'clock the following morning – but later, when Green checked the body, he found that the poor old soldier had passed away.

1893 The findings from a Gainsborough inquest, regarding the body **30 JANUARY** of Ann Boyes (66), were published. Ann's husband, James, a seedsman of Bridge Street, had last seen his wife shortly before he went to bed at 11 p.m. She had been in low spirits and had been drinking, but, he said, not to excess. Emma Whitlam, another witness, stated that when James had gone away on business, Mrs Boyes had pawned some of his clothes for drink money. Ann had done this before. She had previously worried about the trouble she would get into with her husband for pawning his clothes, and had threatened to 'make away with herself' on more than one occasion. However, this time, the following day, the body of Ann Boyes was recovered from the River Trent near the Sailor Boy pub. The inquest returned the verdict 'found drowned'.

1889 An accident was reported at Hornsby's Agricultural Implement **31 JANUARY** Makers in Grantham. Harry Gace (19), who lodged in North Street, was working in the running shop as a machinery assistant. His job was to keep the machinery clean and well oiled. Tragically, while he was lubricating a wheel, he became caught; before he could be extricated, he had been drawn in, causing multiple fractures to his ribs and reducing his left arm to a pulp. Gace was conveyed, in an unconscious state, to Grantham Hospital as quickly as possible, and was attended by three doctors – but they all agreed that it was almost impossible for him to recover.

Grantham Hospital.

FEBRUARY

King George III.

The Madness of King George III

Ordained priest and physician Francis Willis (1718-1807) moved to Greatford Hall, near Bourne, in 1776. He developed the house and grounds as a private rural sanatorium. Here, Willis's methods of treatment included blistering of the skin, coercion, and restraint in both straitjacket and a specially adapted chair. He also promoted fresh air and manual labour as therapy, encouraging his patients – irrespective of their rank or status – to perform work in the stables and grounds of the estate. In 1788, Willis treated King George III. His Majesty was suffering from a madness (now thought to be a condition known as porphyria), but was not excused from any aspect of Willis's regime. In February 1789, when Willis announced the 'entire cessation of his Majesty's illness', his reputation was made. The King granted him £1,000 a year for twenty-one years.

1850   An old country tradition, which helped to maintain law and order, was the shaming of men who became a cuckold or mistreated their wives, or those who overtly transgressed the rules of marriage, by making them 'ride the stang'. This involved a roughly made wooden horse that would be ridden backwards around the village by the offending male in quite a public spectacle, accompanied by 'rough noise'. Remnants of this old tradition were far from dead in Louth in 1850 when John Williams, a local dealer in old clothes and miscellanea, became possessed with a jealous mania and assaulted his wife and daughter. He then dragged his wife out of bed by the hair on her head. When news got out of what he had done, a group of youths rang a warning peal by making 'rough noise' in the finest tradition, upon sundry old pans and kettles, and shouted remonstrations. John Williams was arrested, along with one of the noisy urchins. Williams ended up in court and was fined 10s plus costs for the assault, and was ordered to enter into his own recognisance. He had to find two sureties of £25 each, assuring his good behaviour to his family for the next six months. The urchin boy was discharged by the Superintendent of Police.

1886   The case of William Kirchen was reported. Kirchen, who had been committed for trial on charges of murder, appeared before Lincoln Assizes on the reduced charge of the manslaughter of Harriet Hoe, his stepdaughter. The previous October, Kirchen had returned home drunk and an argument with his wife had ensued. Harriet had gone to bed but then returned downstairs to intervene. Her mother ran out of the room and Kirchen lashed out at Harriet, throwing a lit paraffin lamp at her. The lamp smashed against the wall but burning oil had splashed over Harriet, causing her such burns that she subsequently died. Kirchen did try to extinguish the flames, and both his wife and stepdaughter (before she died) spoke up for him. Kirchen was sentenced to three months' imprisonment with hard labour.

1879   On this day, the Melton Ross railway bridge tragedy occurred. The bridge, located about 2 miles from Barnetby Junction, was wide enough to span the Manchester, Sheffield and Lincolnshire main lines, and formed a portion of the high road between Brigg and Brocklesby. The bridge had been considered unstable for some time, and work was begun to demolish it and build anew. A wooden scaffolding was erected, and blasting powders were put in seventeen places across the bridge. These were blown but without the desired effect, so the workmen began to pull down the bridge manually. The superintendent of the works warned the men that what they were doing was dangerous, but they carried on. At about 3.30 a.m., as the men worked by the light of oil lamps, a hole was made in the crown of the arch where about a dozen men were working. Without warning, the entire arch fell in, taking men and scaffolding with it. A vast pile of debris resulted and the air was filled with the shrieks and moans of the maimed and wounded men. It took until 10 a.m. to extricate all the bodies from the rubble and wreckage. Robert Jobson, Ellis Hornsby, Edward Ambler and Thomas Robinson were all found dead; twelve more were badly injured; and many more suffered minor cuts and bruises, and were assisted to their homes. The dead were conveyed to Barnetby station and were placed in the waiting room. The inquest was held at the Station Hotel before Mr F.B. Cousans, the deputy coroner. After hearing the evidence, the jury returned a verdict of 'accidental death' in all cases.

4 FEBRUARY   1847   Charles Stewart, the notorious Chartist agent who had been tried along with Feargus O'Connor at York, was reported as having been committed to Lincoln City Prison on a charge of bigamy. He had married Miss Caroline Harrison of Lincoln when he already had a wife, whom he had married in Scotland in 1837!

5 FEBRUARY   1891   An inquest was held at Spalding touching the death of Jonathan Grundy (67), a well-known agriculturalist in South Lincolnshire who had recently retired. Grundy had been seen the previous night acting strangely and making particular enquiries as to the running of trains. The following morning, his remains were described in press reports as being found 'scattered about the Great Eastern Railway line near his own house, the body being literally cut to pieces and frightfully mangled'. The inquest jury returned a verdict that the deceased had wandered onto the line while temporarily insane and was killed.

6 FEBRUARY   **Punishments of the Past: Branding**
Branding, a term from the Teutonic word *brinnan*, 'to burn', was used by the Anglo-Saxons until the nineteenth century. The punishment was carried out by the application of a red-hot branding iron to the hand or face. The letter you were branded with depended on your crime: 'V' for vagabonds; 'T' for thieves; 'C' for coin-clippers; 'B' for blasphemers; 'S S' (One 'S' either side of the nose) for those who sowed sedition; 'M' for malefactors; and 'FA' for false accusers. In 1726, prisoners who could demonstrate their ability to 'read like a clerk' were not treated as common criminals but had the right to be cold-ironed, whereby, on payment of a small sum, the branding iron was plunged into cold water before being pressed against the skin.

7 FEBRUARY   1855   At about 3.30 p.m. a fire broke out in a barn belonging to Charles King of Coates Grange. The fire destroyed twenty-seven quarters of unthrashed wheat, causing total damages to the value of £250. It was only contained by the prompt action of employees and neighbours, and the timely arrival of two fire engines from Louth. The fire had been caused

Branding a felon.

by a workman, who had examined the shaft of a thrashing machine with a candle. The flame had been drawn upwards by a current of air and had ignited the wheat, which, being very dry, burnt with great fury.

1884 John Price (41), a prisoner at Lincoln County Prison, had been engaged outside the walls for some minor work when he made a bolt for freedom. His escape was noticed almost immediately and a chase ensued, with escaped prisoner and warders crossing hedges and jumping ditches. Price lost his pursuers in Burton. The local police were brought in and Detective Sergeant Hockney and Sergeant Richardson of the City Police were soon on the case, conducting their search for Price by horse and trap. Obtaining a clue at Aisthorpe, they tracked Price down to a cottage kitchen, where Hockney pounced upon him and, having applied handcuffs, returned the fugitive to the prison.

8 FEBRUARY

John Howard Reports on the Prisons of Lincolnshire:

9 FEBRUARY

Lincoln Castle, The County Gaol [visited 1768], Gaoler Isaac Wood, unsalaried but paid a variety of fees from prisoners. He also received £154 a year to supply prisoners with food and to pay land tax. The Gaoler was contracted to keep the prison in good repair. He also brewed his own beer and let the tap. Lincoln Castle itself belonged to the Duchy of Lancaster and covers a spacious area of six or seven acres. On the ground floor are the gaoler's apartments, tap room etc. For Master's side debtors, six sizable rooms on the first storey and as many garrets. The floors of both stories are tarras and cannot be kept clean: the passages only six feet wide, with windows close glazed.

The free ward for debtors is the only room at the end of the building, down two steps. It is paved with small stones and is a thoroughfare to sundry places. First, by trap door in the said pavement, you go down ten steps to two vaulted dungeons for criminals, eight feet high; one known as the Pit, fourteen feet by twenty one, window two feet by fourteen inches; the other within it, the condemned cell, fourteen feet by eight; window about nine inches by eighteen: a little short straw on the floors; both dungeons dirty and offensive. You also pass through it to the Women-felons ward which joins to it and is eleven feet by eight and to the felons small court-yard and their sizeable day room, fifteen feet by nineteen: no water: no sewer and to a room for the closer confinement of debtors who do not behave well. There are two rooms with beds for felons who can pay for them.

No chapel: the service is performed in the Shire Hall. No infirmary. The whole prison is out of repair perhaps because the County designs to build a new one.

... On a tomb stone in the Cathedral, is an inscription, noting that Clement Wood interred there, was thirty three years Gaoler of the Castle and of the city Gaol.

10 FEBRUARY

1882   The case of Thomas Cross (30), a labourer indicted for setting fire to a stack, the property of his brother Edward Cross at Wrawby, was reported. The incident had arisen after Thomas Cross got drunk and came to the stack yard to see a man named Sargent, with whom he had some disagreement. Sargent had knocked Cross to the ground and kicked him. Cross's brother, and another man named Thomas Lankester, had been present but had not intervened. Later that night, Thomas Cross was seen running away from the stack yard and a fire was discovered shortly after. It was soon extinguished and little damage was done. Cross was arrested and blamed his actions entirely on drink. He was sentenced to three months' imprisonment with hard labour.

11 FEBRUARY

Cures of Cunning Folk in Fen and Wold: Charming Warts

A popular method for getting rid of warts in the Fens was to rub them with a raw potato at midnight. When in season, the inside of a broad bean pod, or dandelion juice, could also be rubbed on the wart. Another 'cure' was rubbing the wart with a piece of meat, especially liver – the meat was buried in the garden then, as it decomposed, the wart was said to do similar.

Another cure was to touch each wart with a piece of straw; the sufferer would then close their eyes and throw the straw over their left shoulder. Yet another method was to tie a horse hair round the wart, then anoint it with seven drops of blood from the snout of a freshly killed mole.

If the wart or warts persisted, a professional charmer may well have been consulted. Some would 'sell' their wart to a wart buyer, who would give them a halfpenny which they then had to lose, and then the warts would supposedly disappear. Another method was to rub the warts with a toad or large grey snail, then pass the toad on to someone else, who had to hang it on a thorn bush; it was said that as the toad or snail died and withered, the warts did likewise.

1871 Alfred Cousens was returning to Kirton from Brigg when the mare pulling his cart took fright near Redbourne and galloped off furiously. Cousens was thrown out of the cart near the park gates; the mare continued to gallop into Kirton Market Place. No one could stop her and she only came to a halt after running against the town pump, which was a tall, cast-iron construction with a lamp on top. The only damage to the cart was a smashed front board. The mare escaped quite unhurt.

Alfred Cousens
being thrown
from his cart as
his startled mare
gallops into Kirton.

1855 An inquest was held by George Marris Esq at Grimsby on the body of Jane Marshall, the keeper of a brothel in East Street, who had died suddenly. It had been suggested that her death was caused by injuries inflicted on her in the house a few days previously, but the surgeon's evidence (based on the findings of his post-mortem examination) proved that her death had been caused by inflammation of the bowels. The jury returned a verdict accordingly.

1815 Newspapers reported the arduous feat achieved by Joseph Goodwin jr of Stamford. Joseph had carried a brick, in his right hand, from the Hole-in-the-Wall public house in Cheyne Walk to Ryhall toll bar and back, a distance of about 2.5 miles. This might not sound too challenging. However, what made the task difficult was that he was not allowed to alternate which hand carried the brick, nor to raise his arm so that the sinews could be relieved from cramp, or the circulation of blood assisted. He was allowed to swing his arm, but had to grasp the brick (which weighed 63lbs) constantly in his hand.

15 FEBRUARY **1850** The mysterious death of Mary Dickinson (86) was reported after recently occurring at Bracebridge near Lincoln. The inquest, held before Mr Hitchins, revealed that Mrs Dickinson had lived with her granddaughter Elizabeth Hoe, and that the elderly lady had died from three incised wounds – one extending from under the throat, up the right cheek to the temple. Mrs Hoe stated that the cuts had been caused during a fall down the narrow stairs of the house. Mr Hill, the surgeon, deposed that the wounds had been the cause of death, but said that they could not have been caused by a fall...

16 FEBRUARY **Punishments of the Past: The Cage of Lock-Up**
Up until 1840, every parish was required by law to provide a 'lock-up' or cage for the temporary detention of prisoners arrested by the parish

Digby Lock-up.

constable. These were usually small wooden and brick structures, about 8 or 10ft square, built on waste ground in a public part of the village. The lock-ups were often in close proximity to the stocks and whipping post. A number of cages and lock-ups still exist in the county, with good examples to be found at Deeping St James and Digby.

1817   The findings of an inquest on the death of Elizabeth Housman **17 FEBRUARY** were published. Housman was a servant in the employ of William Swift. When caught fraudulently conveying away some property belonging to her master, she destroyed herself by drinking a solution of arsenic, commonly known as fag-water. The efforts of medical men to restore the wretched woman failed and, after lingering for several days in great suffering of mind and body, she died. The jury returned a verdict that she had destroyed herself while suffering a fit of 'mental derangement'.

1871   Christopher Leedham (65), a Stallingborough brick maker, **18 FEBRUARY** had been a widower for some time, and his five children had grown up before he had married a woman twenty years his junior. The children seemed to have accepted the situation but, following an internal injury, Christopher's eldest son George (36) suffered a worrying irritability of temperament. During the course of their evening meal, as his stepmother was serving rice pudding, George began to eat the pudding from the dish with a knife. She told him not to do so. With a snap retort, 'I shan't!', he struck a backward blow with the knife, which entered the lower part of the right side of her neck, penetrating the jugular vein. As she slumped

George Leedham fatally stabbing his stepmother during a family dinner at Stallingborough.

down from her fatal wound, George withdrew the knife, ran out to the brick pond and jumped into the water. Dragged from the water, he was determined to destroy himself; he fought off those who were trying to save him and succeeded in drowning himself. At the inquest on the following Monday, before Mr Marris, the coroner, the jury returned a verdict of 'homicide whilst in a fit of insanity'.

19 FEBRUARY   **1883**   John Anderson was the first man to be executed at Lincoln's new prison on Greetwell Road. Anderson (64) was a retired publican living apart from his wife, Mary Ann (51). The inter-family relationships of husband, wife and son had gone badly wrong, and Mary Ann had brought a case against her son for assault before the Gainsborough magistrates on 5 December 1882. The following day, Mary Ann had gone to the family home to collect her clothes. Angry words had passed between Mary Ann

The entrance gate of HMP Lincoln.

and her husband. Mr Anderson had then got up, locked the door and struck his wife. She had run into the back kitchen, but Mr Anderson had taken a knife out of his pocket and followed her in; a struggle ensued. A nephew, with whom Anderson had been having dinner at the time, had fled the house to raise the alarm and, shortly afterwards, he and a neighbour saw Mrs Anderson stagger out with blood pouring from her throat. The neighbour had taken hold of her, and she had managed to walk a few paces to the Ferry House pub where, in the doorway, she collapsed and died. The post-mortem revealed that her jugular vein had been severed. Anderson was found in the house; he had attempted to cut his own throat but his cut was not as severe. He was given medical treatment and later recovered sufficiently to stand trial at the Lincoln Assizes. Anderson showed little concern, and was even heard to laugh while the jury were considering their verdict. Found guilty, Anderson was sentenced to death and was executed by William Marwood.

Strange Tales and Folklore of Lincolnshire: The Tiddy Mun

20 FEBRUARY

Lincolnshire has no shortage of stories of 'Tiddy Ones', the little people or fairies. Probably the most feared of them all was the Tiddy Mun – the

A carved stone grotesque on one of the churches in the land of the Tiddy Mun.

Little Man – said to be about the size of a toddler but with the wizened appearance of an old man, with long, tangled white hair and a matted white beard. He wore a grey gown so that at dusk he was difficult to see, and his laughter was said to resemble the call of the peewit. The Fen folk bitterly resented anyone who attempted to change their wetlands, and woe betide any engineer or navvy who lingered there after dark. The Tiddy Mun was blamed for the deaths, or sudden disappearances, of those who laboured for the drainage engineers of the Fens between the seventeenth and nineteenth centuries.

21 FEBRUARY **1887** Richard Insole was executed at Lincoln. Insole was a Grimsby fisherman who had been sentenced to six weeks' imprisonment for assaulting his wife, Sarah. He had been summoned initially for refusing to support her. In a final confrontation at her parents' house, she had refused to resume cohabitation and Insole had fired five shots at her – two when she was on the floor. He had then stabbed himself in the groin. Sarah Insole died ten minutes later. Richard Insole recovered and was brought before Lincoln Assizes, where he was tried, found guilty and sentenced to death. James Berry was the executioner and it was recorded that Insole 'appeared to meet with instantaneous death. Not even a quiver of the rope could be observed'.

22 FEBRUARY **1899** Incendiarism was reported on a Crown farm in Holbeach Marsh, which was occupied by Henry Cole Tinsley. The fire took over fourteen hours to bring under control; twelve calves were lost, along with stacks of wheat straw and two valuable clover stacks. The damage caused was estimated to be around £2,000. Spalding Police were also challenged by the discovery of human remains in the debris of the fire. An investigation was launched to establish the identity of the body; it was thought to be that of a tramp who had been sleeping in one of the stacks and had inadvertently started the fire.

23 FEBRUARY **Tales of Lincolnshire Smuggling: The Mablethorpe Owlers**
Mablethorpe was a hotbed of smuggling in the eighteenth and early nineteenth centuries, with people from all strata of society in the community 'in the know'. The locals made an art of 'foxing' the excise men by luring them to one part of the coast by lantern lights or false information passed to them 'in secret and confidence' as good, while the smugglers landed their cargo unopposed elsewhere. The locals were also not averse to giving a few drinks to the coastguards, keeping them in the pubs and away from their duties; such a ploy was not cheap. Local farmers hid the contraband in their carts, covered by 'taties'; they would always make sure to 'put a guinea in both eyes' of an official so he would see nothing.

Strange Tales and Folklore of Lincolnshire: Death of a Maiden

Mary Hill died whilst ringing one of the four bells at Springthorpe church on Shrove Tuesday in 1814. By accident, she had been drawn up to the roof and had then fallen to the floor, hitting a large stone that now forms the base of the font. Three Maidens' Crowns, three garlands and three white gloves were carried at her funeral by three maidens dressed in white. As she was unmarried, these symbols were a mark of her chastity. Only one of these Crowns remained by the 1890s, and is displayed in a glass case within the church. A loyal replica of the old Maiden's Crown now hangs in its place. An old verse in the church concludes:

Six maidens all in white
Did bare her to the grounds
The bells did ring in solemnsori
And made a solemn sound

In earth they laide her there
For hungry worms a preye
So shall the fairest face alive
At length be brought to claye.

The Maiden's Crown.

Springthorpe
church.

25 FEBRUARY   **1893**   Caroline Sharpe (36), a dressmaker who lived on Lincoln High
Street, was charged on remand at the City Sessions House, Lincoln, with
the wilful murder of Eliza Ann Luff. She had performed an illegal operation
(an abortion) upon the latter. Sharpe may well have been carrying out this
practice for quite some time before the death of Eliza Luff, who had gone
to Sharpe of her own free will. Luff had returned home afterwards but,
racked with pain, had called in her doctor. Realising all was lost for her, she
had confessed what she had done before she died. At the trial, the judge
explained to the jury that, apart from the dying declaration of Luff, which
he felt bound to say was inadmissible, there was no evidence to convict the
prisoner. Caroline Sharpe was accordingly discharged on this day.

26 FEBRUARY   **1889**   The most serious fire to take place in Spalding occurred on this
day, in a large granary rented by Messrs F.C. Hopkins & Co. The granary
was attached to a steam corn mill on the High Street, and was being
used to store dry timber. The fire spread rapidly and was so intense that
the local fire brigade was unable to save the building. Instead, they
concentrated on containing the fire and stopping its spread to other
nearby buildings. In the light of the morning, only four bare walls of the
gutted warehouse were standing. The damage was estimated at between
£3,000 and £4,000. The cause of the fire remains undiscovered.

27 FEBRUARY   **1817**   An alarming circumstance was reported in Brigg. A young
person by the name of Mann, an apprentice to Mr Pape, a millwright,
used a composition of soft soap and roll brimstone to cure an itch – he
died soon after its application. At the inquest, a surgeon stated his opinion
that the death of the young man had been accelerated by the soap and
brimstone, which had been applied in consequence of another disease
under which the deceased was then labouring – the fruit of his dissipated
habits. This statement will no doubt serve as a caution to others.

1850 At an inquest held at Trent Port Inn, Gainsborough, John Raynor and Henry Anders testified that they had been looking for pike in some water known as the Delph, when they found a basket floating on the surface containing the body of a child aged about 3-4 weeks. Upon inspection, the body was found to be wrapped in old linen and a piece of newspaper. Mr Cook, the surgeon, carried out the post-mortem and deposed that he found no marks of violence upon the body; he could not ascertain the cause of death and so a verdict of 'found dead' was recorded.

Cures of Cunning Folk in Fen and Wold: Opium

For centuries, the Fen folk were plagued with ailments such as malaria, rheumatism, asthma and ague. A universal 'cure all' was to drink, or eat the seed of, the great white opium poppies that grew in profusion across fenland. Some labourers frequently took poppy-head tea for their meal breaks, probably to relieve the daily drudge. This potent brew was used to delay the onset of labour by mixing it with gin; it was even used as a tincture to quiet and sooth teething children! As the old couplet stated:

> Poppy Tea and Opium Pill
> Are the Fen cure for many an ill

In the mid-nineteenth century, it was said that there was not a labourer's house without its penny stick or pill of opium, and not a child that did not have it in some form. According to an analysis made in 1862, more opium was sold in Cambridgeshire, Lincolnshire and Manchester than in any other part of the country. Some addicts were known to take anything between 40 and 90 grains a day (about 30 grains could be bought for a penny). Some areas were worse than others; Crowland was known for its 'Opium Slaves' and Spalding had a reputation as an opium-eating town in the 1820s.

The opium poppy, once common to the Fens.

One man in South Lincolnshire told a reporter that his wife had spent £100 on opium since they had married. Other addicts were observed too:

A man may be seen occasionally asleep in a field leaning on his hoe. He starts when approached, and works vigorously for a while. A man who is setting about a hard job takes his pill as a preliminary, and many never take their beer without dropping a piece of opium into it. To meet the popular taste, but to the extreme inconvenience of strangers, narcotic agents are put into the beer by the brewers or sellers.

You certainly had to watch what you drank in Lincolnshire past!

MARCH

The tower of St Botolph's Church, Boston, *c.* 1905.

Strange Tales and Folklore of Lincolnshire: Boston Stump

A tragic scene is occasionally re-enacted in ghostly form upon the 272ft-high tower of St Botolph's Church, commonly known as Boston 'Stump'. On autumn evenings, the ghost of a young woman named Sarah Preston, with her young child in arms, is seen to fling herself over the parapet and hurtle silently towards the ground before disappearing. One story attached to this haunting is that poor Sarah was blamed for bringing plague to Boston, and took her life, and that of her child, rather than face the wrath of the local people.

1 MARCH **Strange Tales and Folklore of Lincolnshire: The King's Champion**

From the fourteenth century, the position of the King's Champion was held by successive members of the Dymoke family of Scrivelsby. The duty of the office was to ride into Westminster Hall at the Coronation banquet and challenge anyone who impugned the King's title. During the Wars of the Roses, the struggles for the throne meant that the Dymokes did not always have a clear candidate for their loyalty.

Sir Thomas Dymoke's father had been champion for Henry IV, and thus he gave his support to the Lancastrians. He helped his brother-in-law, Sir Robert Welles, raise an army of 30,000 men in Lincolnshire for King Henry VI. Hearing of the force raised against him, Edward IV marched his army to Lincolnshire and defeated Sir Robert's army near Stamford on 13 March 1470.

Reprisals were swift; Sir Robert was beheaded on the battlefield, and, a few hours later, his father and Sir Thomas Dymoke met the same fate in London at the hands of the executioner.

Defending the honour and right of the King.

1877   Samuel Sewards, a farm servant of Ferry Corner Plot, was charged by his master, Samuel Barnes, with stealing oats to feed his own horses. Sewards acknowledged his offence. His employer gave him a very bad character and the magistrates committed him to Spalding Prison for twenty-one days' hard labour.

2 MARCH

1817   An inquest was held at Leeds Gate Inn, near Boston, upon the body of Elizabeth Inman (72), who had been found drowned in a well belonging to the inn. It appeared, from the testimony of her husband (who had been blind for some years), that they had been in bed the previous Friday night when Mrs Inman got up to go to the privy. Because she was gone quite some time, Mr Inman had grown concerned. He had informed the ostler at the inn, who had conducted a search and discovered Elizabeth in the well. A belief was entertained that the deceased had had a quantity of old silver coins in her possession, and dared not get them exchanged for fear that the parish officers, on hearing of it, would stop their weekly allowance. This, people surmised, had played so heavily on her mind as to induce her to destroy herself. However, the coroner suggested that it was just as likely that she had fallen in by accident, and recommended that the jury should take her age and infirmity into consideration. A verdict of 'found drowned' was accordingly returned.

3 MARCH

John Howard Reports on the Prisons of Lincolnshire:

4 MARCH

Gainsborough Bridewell [visited 1776]. Three rooms: a small yard: no water: no straw: no allowance: no work. Prisoners are conveyed to Quarter Sessions at Keeper's expense. His salary £30. No Fees. Might be improved on the Keeper's garden.

Cures of Cunning Folk in Fen and Wold: Coughs and Colds

5 MARCH

The most widely accepted treatment for a severe cold – and even whooping cough – was cooked mice. Some children were fed a mouse on a regular basis on the belief that it warded away sickness. A less unpleasant cure was for the sufferer to wear shredded garlic in their sock while they slept.

Another treatment for whooping cough involved obtaining a green 'tossel' from a wild rose brier and hanging it up in the house. Alternatively, plucking a hair from the back of a sufferer's head, then tying the hair to a dog's collar, was said to transfer the sickness to the unfortunate animal.

If the sufferer preferred an equine cure, they could inhale the breath of a stallion, or rub along the body of an old horse. Just in case the transferred sickness killed the animal, sufferers were not supposed to use a good one.

In cases of diphtheria, a gargle with ordinary paraffin was thought to do the trick.

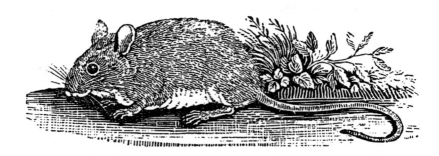

The mouse – fried, boiled or baked – was a Fenland cure for coughs and colds.

6 MARCH 1893   An inquest was held in Boston upon the body of Jonathan Robinson (73). Poor Mr Robinson had suffered from fits of depression ever since his wife died two years previously. Six months before his death, he had attempted suicide by cutting his throat. At the inquest, witnesses stated that he had been drunk on the Saturday night and was always more depressed after he had been drinking. On the Sunday morning, local chemist Robert Munkman had been out walking with a friend on the North Forty-Foot Drain when he saw a man jump in. Munkman had dived in while his friend had summoned help. Mr Robinson proved to be very heavy and was rescued from the water with difficulty. All attempts at artificial respiration failed. The jury returned a verdict of 'suicide while in an unsound state of mind'.

7 MARCH 1851   Robert Meggitt (74) was indicted at Lincoln Assizes for the murder of George Sinderson. The events that led to the trial dated back to the evening of 7 October 1850. When most of the household had gone to bed, a sudden great noise had erupted, and family members and neighbours had come running in to find Robert Meggitt 'quite crazed', with tongs in his hand, threatening to beat someone's brains out. Initially, Meggitt's sons had disarmed him and managed to hold him down. A neighbour, Robert Morley, had told the boys to get dressed while he held down Meggitt. Morley was soon joined by George Sinderson, who used a lot of violence and threatened to shake Meggitt dead if he did not quieten down. Meggitt had complained of choking and wished to get up; this he was allowed to do but, on being released, he drew a clasp knife from his pocket and stabbed Sinderson. Mr Wilkinson, the surgeon, was called and found Sinderson with such a wound to his abdomen that his bowels protruded. Sinderson had lingered for another two days and had then died from the wound. After his arrest, Meggitt stated, 'I dreamed a dream last night that I should kill someone with that knife.' Meggitt was convinced that he had behaved within his rights and stated, 'I am not afraid to meet any magistrate as I consider myself justified in what I have done.' When all evidence had been presented, the jury returned an acquittal on the grounds on insanity.

1893   In a case all too common in the late nineteenth-century police
courts, Henry Holland (42) was brought before the Boston Police Court
for assaulting his wife. The couple had been married for twenty years and
had eleven children, eight of whom were living. On 2 March, Holland
had given his wife 9s housekeeping but, when they went upstairs to bed,
an argument had erupted and he had asked for the money back. She had
returned the money but he had abused and threatened her all night.
The following morning, she had fled to a neighbour's house. Holland
had followed her and pulled her out by the hair on her head. His wife
and a neighbour confirmed that she had suffered many assaults at his
hands, and that she had applied for a judicial separation. Superintendent
Bellamy confirmed that the man had 'ill-used his wife for years'. Holland
defended his actions by saying that his wife drank. The Bench had heard
enough and sentenced Holland to twenty-eight days' imprisonment with
hard labour, granted a separation, and ordered Holland to pay 5s a week
for the support of his family.

1833   During the evening, William Taylor (21) played cards with
William Burbank in a beer-shop in Heckington; Burbank left with plenty
of winnings in his pocket. At about 5.45 the following morning, Burbank
was found by John Nichols, lying dead on the Sleaford road. His skull had
been bludgeoned with a hedge stake, which was found nearby, covered
in his blood. Taylor was the prime suspect; witnesses in the beer-shop
had seen him lose a lot of money to Burbank and two witnesses had even
seen him near the scene of crime. Taylor confessed to the crime when
he was arrested. Tried and found guilty, Taylor was hanged on the New
Drop on 18 March, atop the Cobb Hall in front of a massive crowd. Taylor
went to his death with a firm step and no words of remorse.

1903   The Grimsby knife murderer was executed on this day. On
18 November 1902, a fisherman named Samuel Henry Smith (45) and
Lucy Lingard (33) had been drinking since the afternoon, and took more
drink back with them to Lingard's home on Taylor's Terrace, Hope Street.
    Smith and Lingard began arguing and, a few hours later, Smith
lashed out at Lingard's daughter Rose, blackening her eye. Concerned
neighbours came round; they thought they had settled the situation and
left at about 11 p.m. Soon afterwards, however, they heard a scream and
Smith was seen by another neighbour standing over Lucy's body. Rose
then ran out, screaming, 'Murder!' First on the scene was PC Norton,
who entered the building and found Lucy covered with blood. Removed
to hospital, she was found to have been stabbed eleven times, the blows
having rained down on her head, face, arms and chest. She died in
hospital four days later. Tried at Lincoln Assizes, Smith was found guilty,
sentenced to death and executed at Lincoln Prison by William Billington.

A Full, true and particular account of William Taylor, the unfortunate man who was Executed on the New Drop at Lincoln, on Monday the 18th March, 1833, for the wilful Murder of William Burbank, on the road from Sleaford to Boston, on Saturday the 9th March instant.

Give ear unto this horrid tale, good people far and near,
And of a barbarous murder, you presently shall hear,
Committed was on Sleaford road, the truth I will unfold;
A more cold blooded murder, scarce ever yet was told,

In Heckington one W. Taylor the murderer did dwell,
And likewise W. Burbanks, who by his hand has fell,
They had been drinking and gambling, its true what I impart,
And all that time this monster, had murder in his heart.

With cudgel in possession to Burbank then he came,
And stopped him on the road, his hands in blood to stain,
Several heavy blows he struck him, all on his head and side,
Not time to make his peace with God before he groaned & died.

To see the blood in streams to flow from Burbank's head,
You'd think it almost impossible so much for him to have bled,
But soon the villain was taken, and placed in a dreary cell,
For murdering poor Burbank as many a tongue can tell.

Now when his trial did come on, he at the bar did stand,
Like Moses he stood waiting, for the holy Lord's command,
The Judge when passing sentence made him this reply,
You're guilty of the murder, so prepare yourself to die.

You must prepare yourself to die, on Monday on the tree,
When hung the usual time thereon, buried you must be,
May these few lines a warning be, and prove to others good,
That they may ever shun the sin, of spilling precious blood.

William Taylor, aged 21, late of Heckington, laborer, charged by the Coroners inquest with the wilful murder of William Burbank, on the highway between Heckington and Sleaford, in the County of Lincoln.

William Brown keeps a beer shop at Heckington near Sleaford, the prisoner W. Taylor, W. Burbank, B. Medley, W. Nash and W. Cock, were at his house on Saturday the 9th day of March, W. Burbank came to witnesses house about half past two o'clock in the afternoon, he played two or three games at cards with the before mentioned W. Nash, W. Cook, and B. Medley, about 4 o'clock Burbank asked witness what time of day it was, witnesses wife told him it was somewhere about 4 o'clock, Burbank the deceased took out his purse to pay for two pints of ale, which he had lost, and said that he would go get shaved and then call that part of the town over as he went home, and immediately went out of the house; witness should know the purse again, it appeared to have about 20 or 30 shillings in it, the prisoner also saw the purse, prisoner remained about half an hour in the house after the deceased had left it, the rest of the party remained in the house until the prisoner returned about 7 o'clock in the evening. Prisoner said he would make one to play at cards for a quart, played 3 games, on the last game he said he would bet three pence on his game, he would have three pence for the ale, and said he would then go home. The prisoner remained until about nine o'clock, and was then taken into custody. Witness went on the following Monday morning, to a place called the scalp house in the church to see a dead body, it was the body of W. Burbank.

John Nichols is a Wine and Spirit Merchant, residing at Sleaford, he left Heckington on Saturday the 9th of March, to go to Sleaford at a quarter before six o'clock in the evening, about a mile and a quarter from Heckington he observed the body of a man laying on the road, he dismounted and went up to it, he lifted one hand up with his stick, the man appeared to be dead, but quite warm, supposed it might have been an accident, but on turning round he observed a stake laying across the hedge, one end of which was very bloody, it was five or six yards from the body, it was day light, the stake could not have been taken from the adjoining hedge on which it was laying, witness has seen the stake since in possession of the constable of Heckington, witness immediately rode back to Heckington for Mr. Gibbs, a surgeon, they returned to the body together.

Isaac Cooper, is a rag gatherer, lives at Heckington, on Saturday the 9th inst. he went to Mr. Arnold's Mill near Heckington church, about half past five o'clock in the afternoon, met the prisoner W. Taylor, against the gate of the close in which the Mill stands, witness asked prisoner where he was going to at that time of night, prisoner said he did not know exactly just then, but afterwards said he was going a shepherding, prisoner was going Sleaford way, witness afterwards met W. Burbank about 40 yards after the prisoner, witness spoke to him, he appeared to be very little in liquor, was also going Sleaford way. Witness has since seen a dead body, it was the body of W. Burbank.

W. Hilton, is a carpenter at Heckington, left home on Saturday the 9th inst. about six o'clock to go a shepherding, to a close by the side of the turnpike road, leading from Heckington to Sleaford, he met the prisoner W. Taylor a little past six o'clock, a short distance from Heckington town end. Prisoner asked witness if he could tell him of a job. Witness knows Hilton's close, it is fenced with a quick hedge, it is three quarters of a mile from Heckington, part of the hedge is newly plashed, there are several loose stakes.

W. Gibbs, is a surgeon, residing at Heckington, Mr. Nichols came for witness shortly after six o'clock, on Saturday the 9th inst. to go with him to a place on the Sleaford road, where he found the body of a dead man, it was W. Burbank, examined the body, it was quite warm, and witness supposes it had not been dead more than quarter of an hour, the skull was fractured, a hole into which witness could get his finger, was perforated through the forehead into the brain, the lower part of the forehead was likewise destroyed, the nose was driven quite from its proper direction, the bones of which were literally crushed to atoms, the lip was hanging down in a flap, the upper jaw was fractured, the back part of the head was cut, by blows from a round instrument, deceased died from the

effects of those wounds, a large hedge stake is a likely instrument to cause such wounds. Witness was present when prisoner was apprehended, he denied his guilt. When the constable was going to lock prisoner up for the night, prisoner said he would tell all he knew about it, the prisoner said the purse was to be found near the spot where the body was found, on the other side of the road nearer to Heckington, the blood on the hedge stake was quite fresh, it was wet.

Charles Mastin is a Coroner for the County of Lincoln, and lives at Boston, he committed the prisoner, took the prisoner's examination, and cautioned him that any thing which prisoner might say would be brought as evidence against him. Mr. Mastin was here sworn to his signature, and the deposition of the prisoner was put in and read, it was to the following effect : that the prisoner and the deceased were walking on the road together, the deceased began to quarrel with prisoner about the cards and struck prisoner with his stick, prisoner returned the blow, deceased again struck the prisoner, prisoner then knocked deceased down and struck him two or three times, took from him his purse, emptied it of its contents, 2s. 7d. then threw the purse to the other side of the road, Burbank was not then dead, prisoner returned to Heckington, and on his way met W. Hilton, (as stated in Hilton's evidence al ove,) then went to the beer shop kept by W. Brown and played two or three games at cards, (as stated by that witness.)

J. Wilson is a Cooper, and lives at Heckington, went to the place where the murder was committed and a short distance from it and on the opposite side of the road he found a purse which he gave to John Robinson, chief constable of Sleaford.

Robert Squire is the constable of Heckington, and produced a bludgeon, which he had received from Mr. Gibbs a Surgeon. The bludgeon was a piece of white thorn about four feet long, and about the thickness of a man's wrist, the bark of one end was all hewed off and covered with blood, near the end a part of a branch remained, about three inches long, and as thick as a finger, which accounts for the hole through the forehead into the brain, as stated in the surgeon's evidence.

John Robinson, is a constable of Sleaford, and produced a purse, which he received from J. Wilson. W. Brown, the keeper of the beer shop, is then recalled, who swears that it is the identical purse, which he saw in the possession of W. Burbank, on the afternoon of Saturday, the 9th instant.

Mr. Gibbs, being recalled, stated that the wounds he had before described might be caused by the bludgeon now producing by the constable Squire, into whose possession witness gave it. By Squire, he was asked whether the prisoner attempted to shake the crime off himself and place it on to others, he replied yes, the prisoner told him that he was innocent of the murder himself, but he could tell them who it was that had done it.

This was the case for the prosecution. The Learned Judge, then addressed the Jury at considerable length, recapitulated every minute circumstance that was given in evidence relative to this dreadful affair, making suitable comments as he proceeded in order to make every thing as plain and intelligible as possible, the gentlemen of the Jury appeared to pay every attention, and after recalling some of the witnesses to enquire into some trifling matters that did not appear exactly plain, and a few minutes consultation their Foreman with a down cast look, and a faltering tongue, pronounced a verdict of GUILTY ; the Proclamation being delivered the Learned Judge proceeded to pass the awful sentence of Death on the prisoner, who maintained a sullen silence, his lordship addressed the prisoner at considerable length in an eloquent and solemn manner, commenting on the clearness of the evidence, the magnitude of the crime being the greatest that one man can commit against his fellow man, and concluding by beseeching the prisoner to make the best use of the short time allowed him by law, to obtain pardon of his just and merciful God, through the merits of our Saviour Jesus Christ. He then sentenced him to be hanged, on Monday the 19th March instant, and his body to be buried within the precincts of the prison.

William Taylor was a native of Heckington near Sleaford, he has a father living, who has for many years followed the occupation of a carrier, between the Towns of Sleaford, Heckington, and Boston, he bears an unimpeachable character for honesty and sobriety, and is greatly respected by all who know him, we understand he has or rather had three sons, the eldest of whom is we understand a very steady, excellent young man, in fact quite a religious character, the subject of this brief sketch, and his younger brother have for a considerable time led a life of dissipation, and have been almost a terror to the neighbourhood in which they lived.

EXECUTION.—The unfortunate man was conducted from his dreary cell and handed to the Executioner. Being pinioned he was conducted to the place of execution, where he suffered the awful penalty of the Law in the presence of a great number of Spectators, at the appointed time.

Broadside sold after the execution of William Taylor.

1619   On this day, the Belvoir Witches, sisters Margaret and Philippa Flower, were executed at Lincoln Castle. Both girls, and their mother Joan, had been employed as servants by the Earl and Countess of Rutland, at Belvoir Castle. When Margaret was dismissed for purloining food and for neglecting her work, she made no secret of her hatred of the Earl and his family; this hatred was shared by her mother and sister. The Earl's problems began when his young sons, Henry and Francis, fell ill and died. Local people had already muttered concerns that Mother Flower and her daughters were in league with the Devil and had caused the death of cattle. Some even believed that the Flowers had cursed the Countess and caused her to become barren after the death of her boys. The Earl placed the matter in the hands of the local justices and the Flowers were removed to Lincoln Prison.

When questioned, Joan Flower would not confess and, in an effort to prove her innocence, she asked to be brought bread and water. Before taking a bite, she stated that she wished to choke on the food if she was not innocent of the crimes of which she stood accused. Allegedly, the instant she took a piece in her mouth she fell down dead.

Margaret and Philippa Flower confessed that they had seen their mother 'boyle feathers and blood together using devilish speeches and strange gestures' to curse the Earl and Countess. Margaret also said that she had stolen the glove of their master's son, Henry, and given it to

The Belvoir Witches, Margaret, Joan and Philippa Flower, and their familiars, including Rutterkin the cat, from *The Wonderful Discoverie of the Witchcrafts of Margaret and Philippa Flower, daughter of Joan Flower neere Bever Castle: executed at Lincolne March 11th 1618.* (J. Barnes 1619)

her mother, who had rubbed it on the back of her familiar, a cat named Rutterkin. She had then boiled the glove, buried it in the yard, and uttered incantations that supposedly caused the young man to become ill and die. The women stated that they had also taken another pair of gloves, and wool from a mattress given to Margaret by the Countess. Margaret had put the gloves in warm water and blood, and rubbed them on the belly of Rutterkin, saying that the Lord and Lady should have more children 'but it would be long first'.

Margaret and Philippa admitted to having spirit familiars that often took the form of rats, which sucked from their bodies. Margaret claimed that four devils (Rutterkin, Little Robin, Spirit, and one with a black head like an ape) visited her in gaol. During their examination, the Flower sisters claimed that they had been aided by Anne Baker of Bottesford, Joan Willimott of Goadby and Ellen Greene of Stathern, all in the county of Leicester. All three women were taken and examined, during which they too admitted to having visions and to consorting with familiar spirits.

Both of the Flower sisters were brought before the judges at the Assize and, 'on their own confessions', were condemned to death by Sir Henry Hobart, Chief Justice of the Common Pleas. The Earl remained so convinced that his sons had been killed by the effects of witchcraft that it was inscribed on his tomb at St Mary's Church, Bottesford, that both of his sons 'died in their infancy by wicked practises and sorcerye'.

12 MARCH **1831**   John Greenwood awaited his doom in the condemned cell at Lincoln Castle Prison, on this day. Greenwood (29) was a mariner and had been married to the daughter of John Weatherhog for about a year. He had lived with Mr Weatherhog at Theddlethorpe All Saints before moving out with his wife. A few days after the couple left, a man broke in, presented a pistol at the breast of Mr Weatherhog, then struck him with the firearm, beat him to the ground, and hit him several times with a poker. The intruder demanded that the old man show him his money (which he stole) and his boxes (which he rifled through and stole a silver spoon, a buckle, some shot and other articles). The thief then made off. Despite the intruder using a gruff voice, Mr Weatherhog recognised it as the voice of his son-in-law, John Greenwood. Two constables apprehended Greenwood on the road to Hull. When passing over a bridge, Greenwood attempted to throw the bundle he carried into the river, where it sunk. However, when he was searched, the spoon, buckle and shot belonging to Mr Weatherhog were found about his person. Tried, found guilty and sentenced to death, Greenwood was hanged at Lincoln on 18 March 1831.

13 MARCH **1833**   William Stephenson, alias Beckett (21), 'a fierce looking young man', and Thomas Pearson (24) were brought before Lincoln Assizes, indicted for highway robbery. The prosecutor was John Shepherd, a

Winthorpe grazier. On 2 March, Shepherd had been returning home after visiting a pub at Burgh le Marsh, when Pearson had grabbed the horse's bridle and Stephenson had brought Shepherd to the ground with repeated blows to his head using a large hedge stake. After rifling his pockets, removing a silver watch and some change, they had left him unconscious and bleeding on the road. Recovering his senses, Shepherd had raised the alarm and the highwaymen were pursued and apprehended. Brought before the Lincoln Assizes, they were found guilty of the crime. Stephenson, on leaving the bar, sneered at Shepherd, 'I wish your old flesh may rot off your bones.' A sentence of death was passed but was commuted. Pearson was given a prison sentence and Stephenson was transported for life.

1806   Thomas Temporal, aka Tom Otter, was hanged at Lincoln Castle for **14 MARCH** the murder of his wife, Mary. Otter (28), a navvy employed near Lincoln, had married Mary Kirkham at South Hykeham on 3 November 1805.

On 14 March, John Dunkerley had been drinking at the Sun Inn and was lying down in the hedge near the crossroads at the bottom of the long lane from Saxilby. His slumber was broken by the voice of a man saying, 'Sit down, you can rest here.' Bleary-eyed, Dunkerley made out the figure of a man walking over to a nearby hedge, where he pulled out a stake. By this time, Dunkerley was cold sober and he later stated:

> The moon shined on Otter's face and his eyes frightened me, there was such a fiery look in them ... Then he climbed down to where she [Mary] was sitting with her head hanging down, he cried, 'This will finish my knob-stick wedding.'

Tom Otter striking down Mary Kirkham.

Otter then brought down the hedge stake with mighty force upon Mary, who screamed and called on God for mercy. Otter struck her again and, with that blow, Mary was silenced, her body 'a quiver' then nothing more. Otter went to the Sun Inn, where he was arrested later that night. Mary's body was also brought to the Sun Inn and the inquest was held there. A lasting reminder of the incident were the bloodstains that marked the steps of the inn for many years afterwards (and the hedge stake, which was placed on display in the bar). Otter was brought before the Assizes, found guilty and hanged. His body was then removed to a 30ft gibbet and displayed near the scene of the crime.

15 MARCH   **1817**   Elizabeth Whiting had the dubious honour of being the first person to be executed on top of Cobb Hall in Lincoln Castle. Whiting had been a pauper in Kirton Workhouse, and had administered mixed butter of antimony with Bateman's Drops to her infant female child, who had

Cobb Hall, at Lincoln Castle. Public executions were conducted on top of this tower between 1817 and 1859.

been born out of wedlock. The child had been born on Wednesday, had taken ill on Friday and had died on Saturday. Whiting was so agitated in court that she was unable to stand, and nearly collapsed when the guilty verdict was returned and the sentence of death pronounced. Her execution drew a large crowd and, when set upon the scaffold, she vociferously implored the Lord to have mercy upon her soul. After being left hanging for an hour, her body was cut down and was later dissected for anatomical study.

16 MARCH

1900 Findings from the inquest upon the body of William Loughton (67) were reported by the Louth district coroner, Mr F. Sharpley, at Withern near Alford. William Bullivant testified that Mr Loughton had been assisting to thrash a corn stack when, as he was ascending a ladder to the top of the stack, he had accidentally struck his eye with the hayfork which he was carrying in his hand. Loughton had not considered the wound serious, so he'd simply bound the injury and carried on working. The following day, Dr Hurst was called to attend Loughton – who he found in a semi-conscious state. Two days later, Loughton died. A post-mortem examination revealed that the wound had ruptured a small blood vessel, which had gradually oozed out and formed a clot, causing unconsciousness and death. A verdict was returned accordingly.

17 MARCH

1797 Elizabeth Brocklesby was executed in Lincoln. Elizabeth (42) had been convicted of poisoning her husband, William, at Claxby near Caistor. After the sentence of death was passed, Elizabeth collapsed and was removed from the court in an insensible state. She was reported to have remained so until her execution, when she had to be lifted up to the noose. Her body was left to hang for one hour, then was cut down and handed over to the surgeons for dissection.

18 MARCH

1784 Four men went together to the Lincoln gallows on this day. Thomas Wood, Richard Dowind and William Davison all swung for burglary, while Richard Bull joined them for stealing seven sheep at Kirton. On this same day a year later, nine swung on the same gallows for a variety of crimes, such as highway robbery, horse stealing and burglary. A crowd, estimated to have numbered 20,000, came to observe this multiple execution.

19 MARCH

1889 An inquest was held before Mr Clegg the coroner upon the body of Benjamin Boothby, a farm labourer at Butterwick, near Boston. Boothby had been out of work and was in a very depressed state of mind. During a day when his wife was out, he took the children to their neighbour Mrs Gosling and left them there, saying he was going in search of work. When Mrs Boothby returned to her house, she heard a suspicious noise upstairs and, alarmed, she called a neighbour – who went upstairs to find

Mr Boothby lying on the bed with his clothes on, groaning and complaining of feeling cold. He remained in this condition until the following night, when he died. Dr Shepherd and Dr Pilcher, of Boston, carried out a post-mortem examination, and were both of the opinion that the deceased had died of opium poisoning. The jury returned a verdict accordingly.

20 MARCH   **1778**   Edward Dodson (aka Dowson) and Robert Blades were hanged at Lincoln for highway robbery. On the night of 29 November 1777, Dodson and Blades had held up Ancaster butcher Henry Bates. Dodson had pushed his pistol to the butcher's head with the words 'Your money – or you are a dead man directly!' and relieved him of his valuables. Later that same night, the pair had held up Michael Matkin of Fulbeck. Matkin had attempted to outrun his aggressors by urging his horse to gallop, but was shot dead in the saddle. He kept his valuables but lost his life. News of this mischief travelled fast, and the people of the district were in no mood to give quarter to these killer highwaymen. The criminals were caught at Binbrook the following day. At the Assizes, they stood little chance of mercy and, found guilty, they were both sentenced to death. On the scaffold, Blades was indignant, saying that he would not die with his boots on; he kicked them off as the rope was placed around his neck.

21 MARCH   **1777**   On this day, James Lee was hanged at Lincoln. Lee was a habitual thief who had committed a string of robberies across the county – from Boston to Stow Green and Swineshead. At this last location, Lee had hit the jackpot in October 1776, when he stole goods to the value of £50 (the equivalent of almost £3,000 in modern money) from the home of William Hanley. Eventually, Lee was caught and brought before Mr Justice Nares at Lincoln Assizes, where he was found guilty and sentenced to death.

Stand and deliver!

1733 The notorious highwaymen, brothers Isaac and Thomas Hallam, **22 MARCH** were executed. After conducting a number of robberies both on foot and on horseback, the brothers were finally brought in for the murder and robbery of post-boy Thomas Gardiner (19) at Holton Beckering. Posters offering a handsome reward for information were distributed, and the brothers were duly tracked down in London and brought back to Lincoln. Post-boys lined the entrance to the city and blew their post horns as the men were taken to gaol. Tried and found guilty, Isaac was hanged at Nettleham, Thomas at Faldingworth; both of their bodies were gibbeted near the scene of their executions.

1739 William Lomax, Thomas Sharpe and Joseph Binge were executed **23 MARCH** at Lincoln on this day. Binge swung for housebreaking, and Lomax and Sharpe for horse stealing. Lomax had been successful in his thefts on the roads between Lincolnshire and Derbyshire – but it was a risky business, with stiff penalties if caught. Young Thomas Sharpe was so green that he freely admitted to stealing eighteen horses. All three kept their appointment with the hangman.

1900 Reports were published on an inquest held at Holland Fen, **24 MARCH** concerning the death of local character, widow Sarah Pick (82). Mrs Pick had lived all alone and was the possessor of quite a fortune, with properties in and around Boston and some £2,000 in the bank. However, her lifestyle had always been that of a miser. Her home was little better than a hovel and was devoid of all comfort; the few articles that had served her as furniture were filthy, and the ceiling and walls of her rooms were covered by a veil of cobwebs. Her property was checked to ensure that she had not been robbed, and valuables were found secreted about her house – money in an old teapot, a gold watch in the toe of a stocking, and valuables hidden among papers and rubbish. Her body had been discovered when her neighbour went round to visit and found her lying on the kitchen floor, bleeding from a wound to the head. Dr Reckitt conducted a post-mortem and concluded that she must have been seized with some dizziness and have fallen down, causing the wound. The ensuing shock had killed her. The jury returned a verdict of 'accidental death'.

Strange Tales and Folklore of Lincolnshire: Molly Grime

25 MARCH

In the church of Glentham, Lincolnshire, there is a tomb with a figure on top; this figure is popularly called Molly Grime. Molly was once washed every Good Friday by seven old maids of Glentham, with water brought from Newell Well. Each woman received a shilling for her trouble, in consequence of an old bequest connected with some property in that district. In around 1832, the property was sold and the custom was discontinued.

26 MARCH   1877   Poacher William Clarke became the last person to hang at Lincoln Castle. Clarke (alias Slenderman) was out poaching with three other men. Clarke went off with one of them, a man named Garner, to Norton Disney, near Swinderby. Gamekeeper Henry Walker, and some of his men, spotted the poachers and shouted 'Stop!' Clarke turned and showed his shotgun, then fled. As the poachers ran, the gamekeepers gave chase. Clarke turned again and fired at his pursuers – the shot was caught by Walker's knee. Walker later died from the wound and the pursuit of the poachers became a murder inquiry. All of the poachers were soon rounded up, with the exception of Clarke, and it was only with some keen detective work that he was tracked to Lowestoft, from where he planned to escape to the Continent. At the trial, Garner identified Clarke as the killer; he and his two compatriots walked free while Clarke went to the gallows and was executed by William Marwood.

The grave of William Clarke in the Lucy Tower burial ground.

Clarke was the last executed felon to be carried up the fifty-four steps to the Lucy Tower, the burial place for those who died in prison or were executed. Clarke's dog, a lurcher, pined away after the death of the master it had accompanied so loyally. The dog was stuffed and displayed where his master had once sunk many pints, at the nearby Struggler's Inn at the junction of Westgate and Union Road. The dog can now be seen on display at Lincoln Castle.

27 MARCH   1900   Reports were published of the inquest held at Fishtoft before Dr W. Clegg, the district coroner, concerning the death of local farmer George Hornbuckle (58). Witness George Harrison testified that Hornbuckle had failed to get out of the path of a runaway horse in time. He had held on to its head for as long as he could, but the animal would not stop. Hornbuckle had lost his grip, fallen off, and the horse had passed over him – as had the seed drill it was harnessed to. Hornbuckle had died a few hours later from internal injuries. A verdict of 'accidental death' was recorded.

28 MARCH   1832   Spinster, Elizabeth Bruff, was found dead in her apartment in the workhouse at Bilsby, near Alford. She had long been quartered on the parish funds of Bilsby. Despite this, a search of her room revealed £35 in her cupboard (tied up in a piece of old stocking) and it is thought that she had property elsewhere. With the aid of two tame crows and a favourite hen, she had practised in the occult sciences, for which she was famed among the frail damsels who desired to know their destinies. Two of these girls were the last people to see her alive; about thirty-six hours later, she was found lying cold and stiff across the hearth of her apartment. Death was recorded as from 'natural causes', but many believed she had been killed by someone she had cursed.

29 MARCH **1900** Reports were published of an inquest conducted upon the body of William Radford (83) by Mr G.W.G. Beaumont, the Grantham district coroner, at the Chequers Inn, Woolsthorpe-by-Belvoir. Mr Radford had suffered a fit the previous New Year's Day and had been very depressed since. At about 10 a.m. he had been missed by his wife; after a search, he was found down the well. He was removed from the water as quickly as possible but could not be revived. The jury returned a verdict of 'suicide whilst of unsound mind'.

Strange Tales and Folklore of Lincolnshire: The legend of Tom Otter

30 MARCH

After the murder of Mary Kirkham by Tom Otter (*see* 14 March), Kirkham's body was removed to the Sun Inn at Saxilby for the inquest. Eerily, the landlord found that he could not wash away Mary's blood, which had been spilt upon the pub's steps. Then a mysterious thing happened to the murder weapon (a hedge stake that had also been brought to the pub and mounted on display in the bar, as a grim souvenir of the crime). On the anniversary of the murder, the stake disappeared

A wayside gibbet –
a warning to all!

from the pub and was found near the spot where the murder had taken place – 'wet with gore'. Despite securing the relic with iron hoops, staples or a blacksmith's clamp – and the pub being fully locked up and barred – nothing was found that could hold the item. On every anniversary, the same thing happened. Who or what was moving the stake was never discovered. In 1807 the mischief ended when, upon the orders of the Bishop, the stake was burned in the Minster Yard at Lincoln. Even Otter's gibbet was said to be cursed; the body fell from the post twice due to the weight of the irons and, upon falling the second time, crushed a man and killed him. A quizzical local rhyme ran:

> Ten tongues in one head,
> Nine living and one dead.
> One flew forth to fetch some bread
> To feed the living in the dead
> The answer? It's the Tom Tit that built in Tommy Otter's head.

The gibbet eventually blew down in 1850. The wood was made into souvenirs; a chair (made from the post), and some of the ironwork, are now on display in Doddington Hall.

31 MARCH   **Tales of Lincolnshire Smugglers: Waste Locker Baccy**
George Atkinson, Stephen Andrews, Edwin Bray and P. Palmer Bray, all of them firemen aboard the steamship *Grimsby*, were brought before court at Grimsby in May 1869, charged with smuggling. Customs Officer Edward Mumby had come aboard just as the *Grimsby* was about to set out for Hamburg. When searching the waste locker in the engine room, Mumby had found sixty packages of tobacco in waterproof tin cases, hidden between the boiler and the ribs of the ship. The charge was proved and each defendant was fined £100 – a massive amount (equivalent to over £8,000) for a working man in 1899. They were ordered to be imprisoned in Lincoln Castle until the fines were paid.

APRIL

The legendary depiction of highwayman Dick Turpin.

The Most Notorious Highwayman of All

Dick Turpin, the most notorious highwayman of all time, was no stranger to Lincolnshire, and the county featured heavily in the denouement that led to his capture and execution. Turpin was on the run, not only charged with highway robbery but also with murder, and he fled to Lincolnshire from London. He was soon arrested for stealing horses at Long Sutton but managed to escape from his captors into Yorkshire, where he set himself up as an apparently affluent horse dealer using the name of John Palmer – financing his fancy lifestyle with frequent horse and cattle thefts in Lincolnshire. On returning home after a hunt with some of the local toffs, he foolishly shot a particularly fine cock in the town of Brough and was subsequently brought before the local magistrate to explain himself. 'Mr Palmer' had no proof of employment, and enquiries were made into how he earned his money. Rumours started and Palmer was found to have a number of complaints against him in Lincolnshire. He was taken into custody at York Castle. From here, he wrote a letter to his brother. However, the letter was seen by a local schoolteacher who recognised Turpin's handwriting and communicated his concerns over the true identity of 'John Palmer' to the authorities. Turpin was then positively identified; he was tried, found guilty and sent to the gallows on 19 April 1739.

1 APRIL 1872 The first 'Long Drop' execution occurred on this day. For centuries, condemned felons were left to strangle to death on the end of the hangman's rope. For some time, Horncastle cobbler William Marwood had been conducting experiments whereby the rope and 'drop' of the condemned through the gallows trap resulted in a clean break of the neck and a far more rapid death. The first person to be executed by this new method was William Frederick Horry at Lincoln Castle.

William Marwood, the Horncastle executioner and master of the 'Long Drop'.

Horry was a publican who ran a large and successful inn, the George, at Burslem – but he had a fatefully jealous streak in him. He believed that Jane, his wife of six years, was involved in adulterous liaisons. When

MARWOOD the HANGMAN.

she moved out, he took to drinking. Jane and the children had gone back to her father's on Horncastle Road, Boston; this is where Horry found her on Monday, 15 January 1872. All that the household heard was the report of a pistol, and Horry's exclamation of 'I have done for her'. Horry was immediately filled with remorse; he gave no trouble but simply sent a member of staff for the police and then took a lock of his wife's hair, which he kept with him until he was hanged. Horry proved to be a model prisoner; his only desire was to be reunited with his beloved wife in heaven. Found guilty and sentenced to death, he went quietly to the scaffold. When the cap had been placed over his head and the rope around his neck, he declared, 'Lord have mercy on my soul, for Christ's sake.' He then shook hands with the executioner and said, 'Goodbye to all.' The trap fell, all went without a hitch, and a new method of execution had begun.

2 APRIL Cures of Cunning Folk in Fen and Wold: Aches and Pains
Backache was once 'cured' by the sufferer carrying nutmegs in their pocket, and the pain of sore breasts was alleviated with a dung poultice. Rheumatism was prevented by the afflicted carrying a raw potato (even if it was shrivelled beyond recognition) or a mole's foot in their pocket. For the treatment of sore lips and general relief of sore parts of the body, the leaf of a bruised house leek, applied to the affected part, was said to be most efficacious.

3 APRIL Punishments of the Past: Transportation
In the early years of the nineteenth century, there were over 200 offences which could carry the death penalty – many of them quite petty offences such as poaching, sheep stealing or theft. Due to pressure on

the government to abolish hanging, the punishment for more and more offences changed from the death penalty to transportation. Between 1787 and 1868, thousands of male and female British criminals (some under 10 years of age) were transported in prison hulks to Australia. Their crimes varied from petty theft to rioting. Locked in irons and lying in dock for months, waiting for the ship to fill up before departure on the 252-day journey (a journey reduced to 130 days by 1821), most were weak and malnourished before they even left England. As many as a quarter of the passengers would die before the ship reached Botany Bay.

John Howard Reports on the Prisons of Lincolnshire: 4 APRIL

Folkingham Bridewell [visited 1774]. Damp rooms: no chimney: small yard: no pump: no sewer. Yet the Keeper said a woman with a child at her breast was sent hither for a year and a day: the child died. Conveyance to Quarter Sessions at Keeper's experience.

1877   A report was published of the inquest held at the house of Police   5 APRIL
Constable Markham, North Thoresby, before the coroner Dr Sharpley, touching the death of Anthony Stovin (64), who had been knocked down in the village by a dog-cart and had died immediately afterwards. Poor Mr Stovin was very deaf, and had already been knocked down by a conveyance and badly injured the previous year, but had made a successful recovery. Indeed, it was noted that Mr Stovin had had many narrow escapes from being killed, having met with no fewer than thirteen or fourteen serious accidents. The night of his final calamity was very dark, and the deceased, besides being deaf, had frequently been heard to say that he could not see very distinctly at times. No blame was attached to the driver of the cart, who was proved to have been driving in a careful manner and at an ordinary speed.

1899   A report was published of an inquest held in Boston upon the   6 APRIL
body of John Charles Barber, of the Jolly Sailor Inn, Scalp End. It was revealed that Mrs Barber had found a toy pistol in one of their children's pockets, and was in the act of showing it to Mr Barber when the cocked trigger caught against something and the weapon fired, the ball lodging in Barber's thigh. Despite being attended by Dr Wood, and being removed to hospital where the bullet worked its way out, the wound became worse and, alas, blood poisoning set in with a fatal result.

1681   The Great Fire of Caistor began in the house of John Sheriffe and   7 APRIL
spread rapidly cross the village. The Parish Register records:

In ye space of three or foure houres were consumed and burnt down to ye ground, ye greater half of ye dwelling houses, barnes, stables and outhouses in the town, with all ye shops and warehouses (save one Mercer's shop in ye Beast Market). Five and fourty families were made desolate and without habitation.

A number of lives were claimed and the damage was estimated to amount to £6,786. Collections were made for the relief of the victims, and donations were received from as far away as Compton in Hampshire and Bideford in Devon.

8 APRIL 1893 Reports were published of an inquest held at the Bell Inn, Swarby, upon the circumstances surrounding the death of John Birch (50). On the day in question, Mr Birch had spoken to wagoner John Larratt with instructions for his day's work. He had seemed cheerful enough but, just ten minutes later, his wife, Mrs Jane Birch, was heard to call from the crew yard. Larratt had rushed to see what was wrong, and saw Mr Birch lying on his back upon the straw, a gun lying along his body with the barrel pointing to his mouth, his hat about a yard from his head. It was stated that Mr Birch regularly carried his muzzle loaded, and was in the habit of placing it in the manger when looking at the calves. Mrs Birch stated that her husband had been in low spirits for about a fortnight but had not threatened suicide. The jury gave him the benefit of the doubt, returning the verdict: 'The deceased accidentally came to his death, and not otherwise.'

9 APRIL Strange Tales and Folklore of Lincolnshire: Will O' the Wisp and The Cammeringham Light

The balls of white and yellow light – known as 'Will O' the Wisp', 'Jack O'Lantern', 'Jilly Lantern' or 'hytersprites' – are well known across the Fens in the Eastern Counties. Some investigators have tried to explain the strange lights away as insects, moths or even self-igniting natural gas; whatever these strange lights may be, they do still occur. Those who know the Fens always warn people against attempting to walk across the marshes after dark, but the danger is always seen as far more acute when the Jack O'Lanterns are out. One particularly good example of a Will O' the Wisp light – about the size of a bicycle lamp, but floating free in the air – was recorded between the crossroads on Ermin Street (once one of the greatest Roman roads in Britain), near Atterby Stonepit and close to the gate leading to Old Leys Manor. Local folks were once terrified by the light and would divert their route for miles to avoid the area where it had been sighted.

The Cammeringham Light is said to appear out of a cloud of mist and takes the form of a woman, whom some people believe to be Queen Boudicca, drawing a chariot. She disappears almost as quickly as she materialises. This light, like the one at Atterby, also appears only a short distance from Ermin Street.

Strange Tales and Folklore of Lincolnshire: Curious Palm Sunday Custom at Caistor 10 APRIL

The following was recorded in a *Book of Days* from 1878:

> A representative of the proprietor of the Broughton estate comes into the porch of
> Caistor Church during the reading of the first lesson. He then gives three cracks
> with a huge gad-whip, which he then folds neatly up and retires, for the moment,
> to a seat in the church. When the clergyman begins the second lesson the man
> goes to him with the whip held upright, near the upper end of the stock is a purse
> containing thirty pieces of silver; then he must kneel before the clergyman, waves
> the whip thrice round his head, and so remains kneeling till the end of the lesson,
> after which he retires.

The thirty pieces of silver represented the fee paid to Judas for the
betrayal of Jesus, and the unique ceremony was thought to be a relic of
the Procession of the Ass. Sadly, this tradition died out in the nineteenth
century but the whip itself is still housed in Caistor church.

Punishments of the Past: Swimming the Witch 11 APRIL

Lincolnshire has a long history of witches and witchcraft; many local
people would turn to their local witch or wizard for matters of their
health, heart or fortune – but, if times got hard or society became
touched by upheaval and unrest, such as civil war, the local witch was
vulnerable to becoming the scapegoat for any misfortunes that befell her
fellow villagers.

'Swimming' a
woman accused of
witchcraft.

'Swimming' was one of the most basic and public methods of ascertaining 'proof' of a person being a witch. Stripped to an under-shift, the suspected witch would be 'cross-bound' (left thumb to right big toe and right thumb to left big toe) and thrown publicly into the nearest dirty village pond, river or stagnant ditch. They were given three 'dips'; if they sank and drowned they were innocent and eligible for Christian burial. Those who floated and survived the ordeal would face imprisonment, pressured inquisition to reveal others complicit in their diabolical actions, trial and eventual execution.

12 APRIL **1859**   William Green (22), a poor blacksmith, was brought before Louth Quarter Sessions and pleaded guilty to stealing 15 yards of ribbon and a bonnet from traders in Market Rasen. He had intended to make a present for his sweetheart. He was sentenced to six months' imprisonment with hard labour.

13 APRIL **1802**   A curious case was reported. A cat belonging to Mrs Pollard of Stamford had recently produced a kitten with two distinct and perfect heads, two bodies (united), eight legs and two tails. Further curiosity followed when – in her next litter – the same cat produced a second phenomenon of the same description.

14 APRIL **1900**   An inquest was held in Boston before Mr Snaith, the deputy coroner, concerning the death of widow Mary Ann Bringeman (59) of Cheyney Street. Her family had become concerned when nobody had seen her for a while, especially as she had complained of a violent pain in her head earlier. A search was undertaken by her nephew, Philip Roberts, and, at the suggestion of Mrs Young, her neighbour, the cistern in the yard was examined. Opening the lid, Philip probed the waters and felt something suspicious at the bottom. The police were called and the body of his aunt was recovered by Sergeant Barton. Mary was only wearing her nightdress and had been wearing neither slippers nor stockings. Curiously, the opening of the cistern was only 16in across and was found to contain only 2ft 6ins of water. The jury returned a verdict of 'found drowned'.

15 APRIL **1877**   A case of flashing was reported. Joseph Morris, of Gainsborough, was brought before the police court for indecently exposing himself to females on the public promenades of Cemetery Lane, and in a separate incident upon Castle Hill. William Perry was charged for the same offence, committed upon Spital Road. Both were sentenced to three months' imprisonment with hard labour for each offence.

16 APRIL **1832**   William Greenfield (43) and a local rat catcher named Robinson were caught by farmer Robert Chantry Balderson, at Crofts, in the act of setting their dogs after the farmer's ducks. Balderson challenged the men, at which Robinson replied, 'I owe you a grudge and will now pay you for it.' With that, Robinson snatched a rat spear out of Greenfield's hands and struck at farmer Balderson, but the latter deflected the blow with the weeding tool he was carrying. A scuffle ensued, with both Robinson and Greenfield attacking the farmer. Greenfield dealt Balderson a severe wound to the head with the spear. Balderson's man was soon on the scene and secured Greenfield, while Robinson fled.

Later, when asked by the magistrate, Balderson could not recall why he had been attacked, nor what the grudge was – up until the time of the fight, he was still employing Robinson to kill rats on his premises. Greenfield was brought before the Assizes for the assault and was found guilty; he had been convicted of crimes on more than one previous occasion and was sentenced to be transported. Greenfield was told by the judge that he should 'expect to leave this country now for life'. He was sent to New South Wales aboard the *Camden* and never did return to these shores.

1877   Sarah Booth, a tramp, was brought before the magistrates at Barton, charged with unlawfully wandering about and begging alms. PC George Swinscoe proved the case and she was committed to Lindsey Prison at Lincoln for twenty-one days.   **17 APRIL**

1900   On this day, there was a Board of Trade inquiry at Grimsby upon the death of Arthur Locking (30). The evidence was clear and conclusions were simple. The deceased had been suffering from delusions during the voyage, in consequence of excessive drinking, and had jumped overboard.   **18 APRIL**

1878   The fate of a highwayman, Patrick Fullan, was reported. Fullan had been brought before the Quarter Sessions for Lindsey, held at Lincoln Castle, for attempting to rob Amos Taylor at Laceby. Taylor had been driving from Grimsby when his horse was topped on the road by Fullan and, despite using his whip upon him, Fullan had stayed his ground. Taylor had then leapt out of his vehicle to remonstrate with Fullan and a tussle had ensued. Fullan argued that he had merely remonstrated with Taylor for almost running him over. The jury were not convinced by Fullan's story and found him guilty. Fullan then admitted to a previous conviction and was sentenced to twelve months' imprisonment with hard labour.   **19 APRIL**

1900   Inquiries were made by Gainsborough Borough Police into the apparent disappearance of Joseph Wayman (44), the captain of the keel *Mildred*, which was then lying at Furleys Wharf, Gainsborough. Wayman had last been seen by John Dickenson, a sailor on the steam tug *Bee*, at the Hickman Arms Inn. The following day, one of Captain Wayman's shoes was found under the wharf...   **20 APRIL**

21 APRIL, **1894**   During the second half of a match between the Sleaford Ramblers and Helpringham FC, the ball was kicked out from the centre of the field and landed close to the Sleaford goal. William Hannoth (30) rushed towards it. The Sleaford goalie kicked the ball over the boundary and Hannoth collided with a Helpringham forward named Garton. Garton stumbled over the goalie's back and pitched onto his head, while Hannoth collapsed to the ground, gasped for breath and expired. It was initially thought that Hannoth had broken his neck, but Dr Welchman of Heckington gave his opinion that death was due to the rupture of the heart.

The deceased had been playing under an assumed name because his wife objected to him playing football.

22 APRIL, **1878**   It was reported that the county magistrates at Grantham had five cases brought before them under the Food and Drugs Adulteration Act (1875). In one case, gin had been watered down to below forty per cent under proof; in another, mustard was found to be only four parts out of nine mustard, with the rest made up of a variety of substances, including dried flowers and fine sawdust. A 4lb loaf was found to have so much alum in it as to be injurious to health! These cases were far from unique at the time; food adulteration was inflicted on a vast array of groceries and drinks. This crime was truly despised as the goods affected, such as milk and flour, were often the basic necessities for the poorest people. The crime was summed up in this bitter ditty:

> Little drops of water added to the milk
> Make the milkman's daughter clothe herself in silk.
> Little grains of sand in the sugar mixed
> Make the grocery man soon become well fixed.
> Little acts of meanness, little tricks of trade,
> All pass for keenness, fortunes thus are made.

23 APRIL, **1848**   A number of cases, brought before the police court this week, illustrate the seamier side of the town in the mid-nineteenth century.

John Marwood, the keeper of a brothel in Ashwell Lane, was found guilty of being drunk and disorderly in Walkergate and was fined 5s and 11s costs, or fourteen days in prison.

Mary Leaf, the hostess of the Woodman in Eastgate, was charged by William Schofield with striking him violently on the head with a red-hot fire poker. The marks evincing the attack were still clearly visible on his face. Mary claimed that she had struck out after Schofield had called her 'a name most irritating to a woman'. The evidence of this case was not recorded at length, but was described as of 'a disgraceful and disgusting nature'. Leaf was found guilty and fined 12s and 10s costs or one month in prison.

Jane Everitt, of the kilnyard in Walkergate, was charged by Sergeant Ryatt with brawling, making use of the most disgusting language, and causing nuisance and annoyance in the neighbourhood; she was found guilty and fined 5s and costs, or fourteen days in prison in default.

1878 The case of Elizabeth Walker was brought before the Lincolnshire **24 APRIL** Quarter Sessions. She had been to the shop of George Stephenson, a bootmaker of Crowle, and was spotted by his wife secreting a pair of boots into a 'pocket' she had formed by looping her dress up in front. Mrs Stephenson had confronted Walker on the street and saw to it that she was taken into custody. Walker blamed her actions on drink, but she was known in the area as an opium eater and her defence counsel argued that she was not fully accountable for her actions at the time. The jury found Walker guilty and she was sentenced to four months' imprisonment and was placed on one year's police supervision.

1848 The tragic case of Mrs Cookson, the widow of the late Dr **25 APRIL** Cookson of Minster Yard, was reported. Mrs Cookson's servant had become alarmed when she'd noticed that her mistress's bedroom door was partly open. Seeing that her mistress had got out of bed, and fearing that something was amiss, she had checked the house, then rushed into the garden searching for Mrs Cookson. Once outside, she had noticed that the bucket for the well had been removed. Help was summoned; a neighbour got into the bucket and was lowered into the well, where the body of Mrs Cookson was discovered. The coroner's inquest returned a verdict of 'temporary insanity'.

1883 Reports were published on the inquest held at the Barge Inn, **26 APRIL** Boston, upon the body of Thomas Townrow Harrison, the overlooker at Messrs Newham & Co.'s Lincolnshire Feather Factory. When Mr Harrison was found to be missing, one of his sons had gone to the factory to look for him. Mr Harrison's body was discovered in the shaft of the Cyclops, a steam-driven machine for cleaning feathers. Assistance was obtained and his clothing had to be cut from his body. It was soon clear that he had been caught up by the machinery, drawn round and crushed to death, the speed being 200 revolutions a minute. His employers were keen to point out that Mr Harrison 'was not required to go into the Cyclops when the machinery was in motion'.

1848 Reports were published of a daring highway assault in Barton, **27 APRIL** suffered by local man Henry Stone. Stone had been returning from Redbourne to Brigg when he was set upon by five young men, who had threatened his life and 'otherwise ill-treated him' as he attempted to cross the bridge. Stone had recognised the leader of his assailants as the son of the Brigg bank manager, Mr Barraclough. The lad was known as 'a terror of the neighbourhood' and was brought before the Bench, where he was found guilty and fined £1 5s for the brutal assault.

28 APRIL   Punishments of the Past: The Pillory

The pillory was an effective and humiliating punishment for seditious speech, dishonest traders, perjurers and sexual crimes, dating back to the statutes of the thirteenth century. In England, pillories were considered so essential by the authorities that towns risked forfeiting the right to hold a market for not having one. Once in the pillory, the miscreant would be seen by all, and would probably have been pelted with rotten fruit and vegetables, mud, excrement and even dead animals, depending on the crime the culprit had committed and the mood of the crowd. The last man pilloried in England was Peter Bossy, for the old pillory favourite of lying under oath. His punishment was carried out on Tower Hill, London on 22 June 1832.

A stand in the pillory before an angry crowd.

29 APRIL   1808   The following notice was published regarding an elopement:

Whereas Thomas Kime of Scremby did, on Thursday 24th March 1808, take away Susanna, the wife of William Standwell of Candlesby in the County of Lincoln, Victualler, and two Children named Thomas and Elizabeth. Thomas Kime is about 29 years of age, stands about 5ft 9½ inches high, round face, small thin nose, light blue eyes, light hair cropt, fair complexion. He had on a light great-coat, dark brown undercoat with yellow buttons, short waistcoat, light corded breeches and shoes tied with strings. Susanna Standwell is about 45 years of age, stands about

5ft 3 or 4 inches high, a good looking woman, fresh coloured but rather subject to scurvy in the face. The son is about 12 years old and can write a decent hand. The daughter is about nine years old and is short-sighted. Susanna Standwell is supposed to have concealed cash, plate, linen and various other articles to the amount of £200 or upwards, the property of William Standwell. They went off in a Post Chaise from Boston in Lincolnshire and have since been seen in London. Whoever will apprehend the above named persons and lodge them in any of His Majesty's Gaols, and if possible, secure the property, by giving notice thereof to William Standwell by letter or otherwise, shall immediately receive a Reward of Five Guineas.

1831 The 'Bottesford Privy Tragedy' occurred on this day. The wooden 30 APRIL floor of the privy at the Bull Inn in Bottesford was located over a vault that was some 3 or 4 yards deep. Fatefully, the floor had been in an insecure state for some time but nothing had been done to repair it. During the afternoon of this day, four children, aged between 9 and 12, went into the privy and were dancing upon the floor when, suddenly, it gave way, taking the children with it. All of them were suffocated in the soil and effluvia before help could be obtained. One of the children was the daughter of the landlord, Mr David Hoe; another was the daughter of Mr Dawn of Breather Hills, who, only the day before, had come to her aunt's house at Bottesford to receive her education. An inquest was held at the Red Lion before Mr Clark, the coroner, and a verdict of 'accidental death' was returned.

MAY

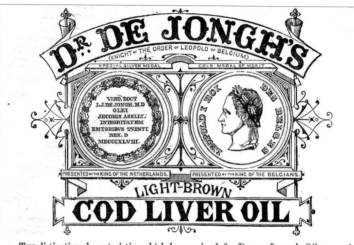

THE distinctive characteristics which have gained for Dr. DE JONGH's Oil so much celebrity, the entire confidence of the most eminent members of the Medical Profession, and, notwithstanding the active and unscrupulous opposition of many interested dealers, an unprecedented amount of public patronage, may be thus concisely enumerated:—

I.—Its genuineness, purity, and uniform strength are ascertained and guaranteed.

II.—It contains all the active and essential principles that therapeutic experience has found to be the most effective in the operation of the remedy.

III.—It is palatable, easily taken, and creates no nausea.

IV.—It is borne with facility by the most delicate stomach, and improves the functions of digestion and assimilation.

V.—Its medicinal properties and remedial action have been found to be immeasurably greater than those of any other kind of Cod Liver Oil.

VI.—From the unequalled rapidity of its curative effects, it is infinitely more economical than any which is offered, even at the lowest price.

Perhaps Mr Jessup should have stuck with a good dose of cod liver oil?

The Heckington Hypochondriac

Samuel Jessup, an opulent Heckington grazier, died on 17 May 1817. According to evidence given at the Lincoln Assizes, it was revealed that, over the past twenty-one years, Jessup had taken 226,934 pills, supplied by an apothecary at Bottesford. Mr Jessup had begun with a moderate appetite, which had increased as he proceeded. In the five years preceding 1816, he had taken the pills at the rate of seventy-eight a day; and in the year 1814 he swallowed no fewer than 51,590. Notwithstanding this, and with the addition of 40,000 bottles of mixture, plus juleps and electuaries, extending altogether to fifty-five closely written columns of an apothecary's bill, Mr Jessup had lived to the age of 65 years. After this, who shall say 'throw physic to the dogs'?

1899   An inquest was held in Utterby, near Louth, touching the death **1 MAY** of Thomas Wright (44). Wright was employed as a drover and had been delivering some animals in Ludborough. On his return, he had met two men taking a wagon-load of furniture from Brocklesby to Keal. These men did not know the road and Wright had agreed to show them the way to Louth. He had climbed aboard the shafts of the wagon and travelled along well enough – until passing near Mr Harrison's house, where he had fallen off. One of the wheels passed over his head, killing him instantly. The jury returned a verdict of 'accidental death'.

Punishments of the Past: Burning for Petty Treason   2 MAY

It is a little-known fact that far more women in England were burnt at the stake for breaching the laws of 'petty treason' than were ever burnt in this country for witchcraft. At the time, every household was treated as a microcosm of the state. The hierarchy saw the head of the house as King, the mistress as Queen, and the servants as minions. The crime of a wife plotting and killing a husband, or a servant deliberately allowing a criminal to enter the house, was classed as 'petty treason', and was punishable by burning at the stake (only a slightly lesser punishment than the retribution for full treason, which was to be hanged, drawn and quartered). The last two women to burn at Lincoln were put to the flames in the eighteenth century – Eleanor Elsom in July 1722 and Mary Johnson in April 1747. Both suffered under the law of petty treason for the murder of their husbands.

1849   A robbery was reported. A man named Stevens, who was **3 MAY** residing in the parish of Bracebridge, was passing the village church on his return journey from Lincoln, at about 10 p.m., when he was set upon by two men – one of whom knocked him down with a stick while the other attempted to throttle him. Only after they had relieved him of his money – a total of some 25s – and his watch, did they flee, leaving him for dead. Mr Stevens was much injured but appeared to be recovering. At the time the report was published, the robbers remained untraced.

1849   British prisons were frequently stricken by epidemic diseases **4 MAY** during the nineteenth century. Outbreaks of cholera, typhoid and 'gaol fever' were rife and, if not contained quickly or effectively enough, would spread rapidly through the prison, infecting prisoners and staff alike. Lincoln County Prison was no exception and, on this day, it was reported that the illness which had 'long prevailed in the prison, has become so thoroughly unhealthy that the prisoners have been removed from the new part to the old that formed the debtors' prison'.

1899   An accident that had befallen William James Price, Professor **5 MAY** of Music at Spalding and the organist of Spalding parish church, was

Lincoln Castle
Prison.

reported. Professor Price and his wife had been out cycling near Holbeach when they had noticed a cow coming towards them; it appeared to be rather menacing. To avoid upsetting the beast, they had dismounted and walked by. Thinking they had gone far enough, they had got back on their bicycles and ridden on. The animal had not been placated, though, and came at them violently. Professor Price's bike had consequently buckled; he was thrown off and rendered unconscious. Mrs Price had quickly ridden for help, which, thank goodness, was not far away. The cow was held off and Professor Price was revived – badly bruised but with no bones broken.

6 MAY   **1899**   In the nineteenth century, some fatal diseases were common to both people and animals. Instances of their outbreak were keenly reported and tough measures were employed to stop them spreading, no matter how hard this hit the farmers. On this day, outbreaks of anthrax were recorded at Kirton-in-Lindsey. The first case was at Ings Farm and, tragically, it spread through fodder supplied to Grange Farm. At the time of reporting, fifteen beasts out of a herd of thirty-three had succumbed at Grange Farm, and a total of twenty beasts from all locations were slaughtered by order of the Board of Agriculture. Compensation for the losses was also revoked.

7 MAY   **1883**   Thomas Garry, known to most as 'Irish Joe', was executed by William Marwood at Lincoln Prison. Garry had been friends with John Newton (74) for over twenty years and had lodged with him at his house in Little Hale Fen since the death of Mrs Newton about eight months previously. Mr Newton was a hardworking farmer, with 13 acres of land,

and he acted as a local preacher for the Primitive Methodists. He was a teetotaller and was not keen on the intemperate habits of 'Irish Joe'. They had argued over this in the past and, on the fateful night, Garry returned drunk from the Wheel Inn and they argued again. In a flash of anger, Garry shot Newton and slashed his throat. He then returned to the Wheel Inn and asked for a bed for the night, leaving for Boston the following morning. By the time of Garry's return in the evening, Mr Newton's body had been discovered. As he walked into the Wheel Inn, the landlord accused him of the murder. Garry replied, 'It's of no consequence. He is as good dead as he is alive.' He was soon apprehended and taken to Sleaford lock-up, and was later remanded to Spalding Gaol. Brought before the Lincoln Assizes, he was found guilty and sentenced to death. This execution was to be the very last carried out at Lincoln by executioner William Marwood. (*See* 4 September)

1845   An inquest was held at Lincoln Castle upon the body of 8 MAY William Howitt, who had been held there awaiting trial on the charge of murdering Mary Spencer, a schoolmistress at Quadring. The attack was said to have been motivated by lust. Her body had been stabbed and 'mangled in the most shocking manner'. A bloodstained suit of clothes, and the knife with which it was believed Howitt had committed the deed, were discovered in a box at the residence of his father. Howitt had been brought up for trial at the March Assizes in 1843 but, being deaf and dumb, had claimed that he was unable to understand the proceedings and was remanded. Evidence at the hearing revealed that Howitt had retained his health in prison, but had eventually begun to betray signs of indisposition and had required medical attention. He was removed to the prison infirmary and 'gradually sank', suffering from diseased lungs and spitting blood. The daily minutes of the prison surgeon were read, revealing that, despite the horrific crime he had almost certainly committed, Howitt was still well cared for. The jury were satisfied and returned a verdict of 'died from diseased lungs'.

1909   Britain was thrilled by the exploits of daring pilots in the new 9 MAY craze of manned flight. In July, Louis Blériot would make history by becoming the first pilot to cross the English Channel – but was he? In May 1909, Britain was gripped by the stories of mysterious zeppelin-like aircraft, which were soon dubbed 'phantom airships' or simply 'scareships', that were seen in the night sky across Britain.

On Sunday, 9 May 1909, the first 'scareship' over Lincolnshire was spotted in the sky over Burghley House, the home of the Marquis of Exeter, at Stamford. A witness, Mr W. Cole, told reporters:

> I was in the park just before 11 o'clock when suddenly I saw a light in the sky over the edge of the woods. It rose and fell seven or eight times quickly, and I saw that

the light came from some dark cigar shape in the sky. The airship, or whatever it was, must have been moving quickly, for first I saw the light on one side of the park, a few minutes later it was on the other side, and then it came back again. I watched it for about ten minutes before it disappeared in the clouds in the direction of Peterborough.

Whether it was mass panic, delusion or real phenomena, the 1909 scareship saga still remains unsolved.

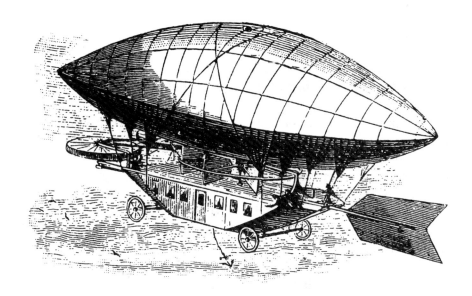

An artist's impression of one of the scareships.

10 MAY **1899** An inquest was held before the coroner, Mr J.G. Caltrop, touching the death of Matthew Mitchell (18), a farm worker of Gosberton Fen. Mitchell had attempted to jump on a train while it was still in motion. He had slipped, and had dropped between the railway platform and one of the carriages. He was dragged a distance of about 15 yards. When the train had come to a standstill, he could not be extricated except by cutting away the footboard to the carriage. This was done, and, despite suffering shocking injuries, the young man had lingered for a further six hours. Death was due to a rupture of the stomach and liver; a verdict of 'accidental death' was recorded.

11 MAY **1886** Henry Taylor, alias George Smith (24), a labourer, was charged at the Lincolnshire Assizes with burglary at Barrow upon Humber, where he stole eight boxes of cigars, 2lbs of tobacco, certain bronze money to the value of £1, and other goods – all the property of John Richardson Simon. Taylor was also charged with assaulting Robert Ailburn, an assistant warder at HMP Lincoln, while in the execution of his duty. Taylor pleaded guilty to both charges and was sentenced to five years' penal servitude.

1811   The following bills were circulated as a warning to the public: 12 MAY

> ESCAPED! From His Majesty's Gaol, the Castle of Lincoln, about three o'clock in the afternoon of Wednesday the 9th day of May by getting over the walls, ROBERT WHARF, a Convict under sentence of Transportation for Life. The said Robert WHARF is about 20 years of age, light brown hair, grey eyes, a round visage, slim made, a good-looking young man, was born at Kirton near Boston; had on a brown coat, strip't waistcoat, blue and drab coloured country breeches and had no shoes on – whoever will apprehend the said ROBERT WHARF and lodge him in any of H M Gaols, shall receive a Reward of Five Guineas from the Keeper of Lincoln Castle.

1855   Thomas Fuller Bacon (36) a whitesmith, invited his mother Ann   13 MAY
Bacon (63) to dine with him at his house at Stamford on this day. During the dinner, Mrs Bacon was seized with a sickness and suffered vomiting and purging for the rest of the afternoon. Dr Barber was called and Mrs Bacon was removed to her own home. She rallied the following day but then declined and died in great pain; her sad death was initially ascribed to natural causes. After her burial, though, tongues began to wag; her son had been in attendance throughout her sudden illness, but his comments that he was confident she would die, and the fact that he had been observed administering something to her out of a small square bottle, aroused suspicion.

Two years later, Mrs Bacon was exhumed and a chemical analysis of her stomach contents was carried out; white arsenic was detected. Brought before the Assizes in July 1857, it was revealed that Thomas Bacon had thought he would benefit from the death of his mother, and crucial evidence of his purchase of arsenic (that he claimed was for 'killing rats in the cellar') was presented. The expert witness was Professor Alfred Swaine Taylor, a lecturer on chemistry and medical jurisprudence at Guy's Hospital, and the author of *Medical Jurisprudence*. He had been present at the exhumation and was convinced that arsenic had been administered – not only because of the detection of arsenic in Mrs Bacon's system, but also from the preservation of her body parts, which he thought 'could only be attributed to arsenic'.

The trial, however, was to have a twist. Bacon's defence barrister, Mr Stephen, argued that there was only a weak motive and there was no direct evidence to prove that Bacon had actually administered the poison. In fact, he argued, the poison could well have been administered by Martha, the wife of the prisoner. Stephen had been present at the couple's trial for the murder of their children by poison (in May 1857) and stated that Mrs Bacon, who had been afflicted by 'homicidal mania', had been acquitted upon grounds of insanity and was currently being held at a lunatic asylum. The judge dismissed this as irrelevant; the jury found Bacon guilty and he was sentenced to death. However, Martha Bacon then

The George Hotel
and St Mary's
Church, Stamford,
c. 1900.

made a statement that she had administered the arsenic herself. After due consideration, Bacon was respited from the gallows and was sentenced to be transported for the rest of his life. Bacon (Convict 6827) arrived in Perth, Western Australia (via Bermuda) on the convict transport *Merchantman* in February 1863, and died just six years later in the prison hospital on 16 July 1869, of 'disease of kidney and urinary passage'.

14 MAY **1859**   A case was reported concerning a gang of poachers. The poachers were on an expedition along the banks of the River Witham, near Washingborough, at about 5 a.m. One of them, Henry Enfield, had the barrel of a loaded gun in his pocket. The gun fell out, struck the ground, and discharged its contents beneath his chin, blowing off the left side of his face and killing him instantly. The train from Boston to Lincoln happened to be passing and the guard saw what happened. He reported what he saw to the police at Lincoln, who located the body.

15 MAY **1900**   An inquest at Boston revealed that Betsy Fox (52) had been suffering from a painful in-growing toenail and had gone to her GP, Dr Reckitt, who had deemed it necessary to operate. She was perfectly willing and had agreed to be chloroformed. Dr Reckitt had called in Dr Belton to administer the chloroform by sprinkling a small amount on a towel, which was then placed over her nose and mouth. In the course of fifteen minutes she became unconscious. Dr Reckitt was about to commence the operation when Dr Belton called his attention to Betsy's features – she had turned pallid. Something was clearly wrong and, despite attempts to revive her, poor Miss Fox passed away. At the inquest, the procedures and experience of the doctors were examined and the jury were satisfied that every care had been taken. A verdict of 'death by misadventure' was returned.

1900 Even in the early twentieth century, epidemics occurred in Britain; one of the most common was smallpox, and families – indeed whole communities – could be wiped out if the disease was not dealt with properly. The afflicted had to be isolated from others to avoid a further spread of illness. On 16 May 1900, when a report was published, five members of one family of hawkers had been taken to the Market Rasen and Caistor Isolation Hospital, where one had already died. 16 MAY

1869 On this day, there was a fatal poaching affray at Cuxwold Hall. In the early hours of the morning, gamekeeper James Marshall and head gardener Enoch Goldney were keeping watch for poachers when they surprised two men in a field at East Ravendale. The poachers took to their heels, with Marshall and Goldney in pursuit. After a chase of 2 miles into the parish of Wold Newton, Marshall lost sight of the other men. The two poachers seized their chance and turned on Goldney, one of them placing his gun against Goldney's head. He fired, killing him instantly, just as Marshall caught sight of them. Marshall summoned the county constabulary, and soon Superintendent Richdale of Grimsby 17 MAY

A violent exchange between poachers and keepers.

apprehended two brothers, Robert (45) and Charles Traves (28), at their home in Ashby-cum-Fenby. Initially, the shotgun used to kill Goldney could not be found, despite a thorough search. However, a month later, a group was employed to weed a field of wheat on Mr Stovin's field in Binbrook; whilst weeding, Mrs Maria Drew caught her foot on the stock of the missing shotgun, which was hidden amongst the ivy near the plantation known as 'Twelve Acre Screed'. The coat worn by Robert Traves was discovered in a hedge. The jury found the brothers guilty of manslaughter and they were sentenced to seven years' penal servitude.

18 MAY **1884** Reports were published of a destructive fire at the premises of Mr Binnington, a farmer, about 2 miles from Binbrook, Lincolnshire. The fire broke out in the stack yard at a time when all of the farm servants were on holiday. It was noted as being one of the largest blazes in the county. The only water available was obtained from a deep well by four men – and proved not to be the slightest use in checking the progress of the fire. The flames spread rapidly from one stack to another, until all eighteen stacks of corn and straw were ablaze at once. On the same day, three labourers' cottages at Fulsover were entirely destroyed by fire. The lack of water there also meant that the entire household furniture, bedding and clothing of the cottages were destroyed and the poor people were rendered homeless.

19 MAY **1884** Reports were published on the inquest held at Epworth Holme upon the body of Robert Hall (30), a farm worker in the employ of Mr Samuel Dixon, who had been found strangled. Hall had been engaged to Elizabeth Hall, a maidservant, and they were due to marry in a few days' time when he was found with a halter round his neck, tied to a tree near the wagon shed. It was commented, 'He was dead when found and was lying face downwards within a few inches of the ground and appeared to have strangled himself with great determination.' His fiancée swore that she had not argued with her lover, and knew no reason why he had done what he did. A verdict of 'suicide during temporary insanity' was returned.

20 MAY **1884** An inquest was held before the deputy county coroner, Mr F. Andrew, at HMP Lincoln upon the body of George Hornby (65), an Epworth labourer who had been committed for trial on a charge of attempted suicide by cutting his throat with a razor. When admitted to the prison, he was still suffering with a partially healed self-inflicted wound in the throat, covered with a bandage. A few days after admission he was found hanging, having tied his pocket handkerchief to the bandage on his neck and then fastened it to a disused hammock hook in the cell wall. A verdict of 'suicide whilst in a state of temporary insanity' was recorded.

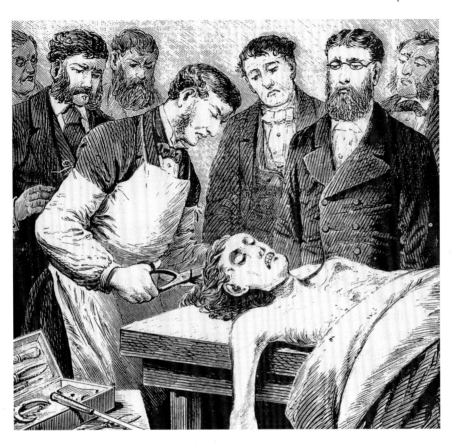

The post-mortem examination.

1877 William Snell Clipstone, farm under-foreman to Mr Calthrop of 2 1 MAY
Horkston Wold Farm, was found to have secreted six bushels of wheat in
two sacks (the property of his master, valued at 5s) in his wagon when
leaving his employment. Clipstone was brought before Barton-upon-
Humber Police Court on this day, pleaded guilty and begged for mercy.
He was sentenced to three months' hard labour in the Lindsey Prison at
Lincoln.

1877 Mary Blayney, a tramp, was brought before the magistrate, 2 2 MAY
Revd Robert Sutton at Brigg, charged with vagrancy. When taken into
custody by PC Fowler, she had acted in the most riotous manner and was
taken to the police station with much difficulty. The Bench sentenced
her to twenty-one days' hard labour at the Lindsey Prison, Lincoln. Her
husband was also brought up on charges of being drunk and disorderly;
he received fourteen days' hard labour.

1887 An inquest was held at the Wellington Inn, Boston, on the body 2 3 MAY
of William Henry Evison (18), a farm labourer. Evison, who had worked
for Mr Mowbray of Carrington, had set out to walk through the night
to his employment. At 6 a.m. he was found asleep on the parapet at the
entrance to the cemetery. When roused from his slumbers, he had set off

in the direction of Boston. He was next seen the following morning in a state of unconsciousness in a field on the Freiston Road, not far from his mother's house. He had evidently slept on cold grass all night. Despite being removed to a nearby cottage, and Dr Tuxford being in attendance and restoratives being applied, poor William died later that morning. There were no signs of violence or any evidence of alcohol. The jury returned a verdict based on the medical evidence: 'Death as a result of coma, the result of exposure.'

24 MAY   1955   On this day, James Robinson was executed. Mrs Mary Dodsley (83) was found murdered in her cottage in Skegby on 16 December 1954. A forced entry through the window revealed a palm print, which led the police to local labourer James Robinson (27). His alibi was that he had been drinking at a pub at the time of the murder; this failed to convince the jury at the Birmingham Assizes and he was sentenced to death. Robinson's execution was carried out by Albert Pierrepoint at HMP Lincoln.

25 MAY   1887   An inquest held at Spalding, upon the body of Edward Mason of Holbeach, was reported on. Mason had unfortunately fallen into the River Welland when drunk. His calls for help had drawn a group of some twenty people to the spot. One young fellow had thrown a prop to him but, by that time, Mason appeared to be unconscious. The coroner commented upon the fact that 'not one of the twenty people had the courage or the manliness to venture into the water which was but five feet deep' to help the drowning man, and that 'not one had sufficient knowledge of swimming to trust himself in the narrow stream'. The jury returned a verdict of 'accidentally drowned'.

26 MAY   1884   On this day, Mary Lefley was executed at HMP Lincoln. William (59) and Mary Lefley (49) lived an apparently quiet life in a small cottage in Wrangle; he was a carrier and she was said to go to Boston market 'and always brought money back' (probably for sexual favours); both were simple country folk. William was aware of, and tolerated, Mary's delinquency for the twenty years that they were married but, as he grew older, he became an intensely religious man and wished to reform his wife. William became so frustrated with her that he admitted to members of his family that he had attempted suicide on a number of occasions. Mary had also been heard to say in exasperation that she wished her husband 'dead and out of the way' – words that came back to haunt her at her trial, after her husband died having eaten a rice pudding she had made for him. The pudding was examined and found to contain a massive 135 grains of arsenic (2 grains would have been enough to kill him). The evidence against Mary was purely circumstantial, but she was found guilty and sentenced to death. When asked if she had anything to say, she replied, 'I'm not guilty and I never poisoned anyone in my life.'

To be submitted to the High Sheriff.

Memorandum of Conditions to which any Person acting as Executioner is required to conform.

———————————

1. An executioner is engaged and paid by the High Sheriff, and is required to conform with any instructions he may receive from or on behalf of the High Sheriff in connection with any execution for which he may be engaged.

2. A list of persons competent for the office of executioner is in the possession of High Sheriffs and Governors : it is therefore unnecessary for any person to make application for employment in connection with an execution, and such application will be regarded as objectionable conduct and may lead to the removal of the applicant's name from the list.

3. Any person engaged as an executioner will report himself at the prison at which an execution for which he has been engaged is to take place not later than 4 o'clock on the afternoon preceding the day of execution.

4. He is required to remain in the prison from the time of his arrival until the completion of the execution and until permission is given him to leave.

5. During the time he remains in the prison he will be provided with lodging and maintenance on an approved scale.

6. He should avoid attracting public attention in going to or from the prison ; he should clearly understand that his conduct and general behaviour must be respectable and discreet, not only at the place and time of execution, but before and subsequently ; in particular he must not give to any person particulars on the subject of his duty for publication.

7. His remuneration will be £ 5   —   for the performance of the duty required of him, to which will be added £ 5   —   if his conduct and behaviour have been satisfactory. The latter part of the fee will not be payable until a fortnight after the execution has taken place.

8. Record will be kept of his conduct and efficiency on each occasion of his being employed, and this record will be at the disposal of any High Sheriff who may have to engage an executioner.

9. The name of any person who does not give satisfaction, or whose conduct is in any way objectionable, so as to cast discredit on himself, either in connection with the duties or otherwise, will be removed from the list.

10. The apparatus approved for use at executions will be provided at the prison. No part of it may be removed from the prison, and no apparatus other than approved apparatus must be used in connection with any execution.

11. The executioner will give such information, or make such record of the occurrences as the Governor of the prison may require.

Memorandum of Conditions for the executioner, sent to Albert Pierrepoint.

Mary Lefley, hanged for poisoning her husband in Wrangle.

She protested her innocence to the end. As she was pinioned by executioner James Berry, she screamed, 'Murder, Murder!' and appeared to be in great agony as she was led by two female warders to the gallows. As the bolt was drawn, she gave a shriek so piercing that it rang painfully in the ears of those near at hand. Did she die with a lie on her lips?

It was suggested that perhaps William had taken his own life by putting the arsenic in the pudding himself. It was also suggested, by Mary's defence counsel, that someone with a grudge against William had snuck in and put the arsenic in the pudding while Mary was in Boston and the pudding was in the oven – but this notion was simply not believed by the jury. On the night before William was poisoned, Mrs Lefley was seen to wink and nod to another man, Frank Reeson. The twist in this tale, so reminiscent of the case of Priscilla Biggadyke (see 28 December), came in 1892. When Frank Reeson lay dying, he was attended by Mrs Daniel Humble. Reeson begged her to stay with him through his last night. With his failing breath, he told her, 'I dare not die with something on my soul.' He confessed that he was one of Mary's lovers and that it was he who had bought the arsenic for Mary. He stated, 'I gave it her, knowing for what purpose it had to be used. Mary Lefley wanted to get her husband out of the way. I helped her. We were false to him.'

27 MAY **1849** George Smith, a prisoner serving twelve months' imprisonment for stealing a box of cutlery from the New Market, escaped from Lincoln City Prison by climbing upon, and then sliding down, the mill. He fled towards Boston in full prison clothes but, despite passing a number of people on the street, nobody tried to stop him. The alarm was soon given and resulted in a hot pursuit. After a great deal of dodging and running, the prisoner was recaptured near Bardney and conveyed back to his old quarters.

28 MAY **1946** On this day, Leonard Holmes was executed at HMP Lincoln. Leonard Holmes (34), who had recently returned from Second World War army service, had noticed that his wife Peggy was flirting with airmen in a local pub. The couple had soon returned to their home in New Ollerton

and an argument had ensued. Mrs Holmes had then openly told her husband that she had been unfaithful while he was away, and said that she was not sure he had been loyal either. She was right – he had had an affair too – but he saw red and killed her.

At his trial, held at Nottingham Assizes, Holmes pleaded provocation and tried to gain a conviction for manslaughter. However, he was found guilty of murder, sentenced to death and went to the gallows, where he was executed by Thomas Pierrepoint.

1920   The Louth flood disaster occurred on this day. During the **29 MAY** afternoon, a huge thunderstorm raged over Louth for about two hours. The storm was so severe that it kept many people indoors. It sent torrents of water into the River Lud (which runs through the town), causing it to rise 15ft in half an hour. Shortly before 5 p.m., just as many families were sitting down to Saturday tea, suddenly, and without warning, the river burst and swept down the town like a tidal wave – carrying away bridges, homes, buildings, cars and people, and flooding many homes in the process. It left a scene of utter devastation in its wake. There were many lucky escapes, but the disaster still claimed the lives of twenty-three people and many more were left homeless. The flood made national headline news; troops were drafted in to help with the salvage work, and the relief fund for the town raised almost £20,000 in the five days afterwards. At the inquest, it was estimated that, in the 20,000 acres in and around the town, the water must have amounted to around 9 million tons and, allowing for ground absorption, it was safe to say that 7.5 million tons of water had passed through Louth in the flood.

People salvaging what they could from the ruins of their homes after the Louth flood disaster.

Funeral of the victims of the Louth flood disaster.

30 MAY   **1835**   An inquest was held at the Black Lion, Chapelgate, Gedney. It was revealed that William Minimack, his wife, and their infant child, had left the Sutton White Lion by horse and cart at about 11 p.m. After a short while, Mrs Minimack had given her husband their child to hold, and she had taken the reins. While travelling at an estimated 7 miles per hour, the horse had flown from the middle of the road and the cart was sent flying towards a ditch. Mr Minimack had thrown the child onto the road and the cart had overturned, flinging Mrs Minimack out; the horse had fallen across her body. Mr Minimack had tried to extricate his wife but believed she was already dead, so he picked up the child and went to

A fearful turnover!

Mr Landens for help. The witnesses only corroborated part of Mr Minimack's testimony. The jury returned a verdict of 'accidental death' but the coroner reproved the 'cool and careless' behaviour of Mr Minimack.

1898   An inquest was held before Mr Stapleton, the Stamford coroner, 31 MAY upon the body of an unknown man who had jumped from the Albert Bridge into the River Welland. Only moments before, an *Evening News* boy had handed him a slip of paper, which he had snatched and put in his pocket before making his fatal leap. A vagrant, who had been with the man in Peterborough Workhouse, said that he had called himself Thompson, and had always exhibited strange behaviour. The vagrant claimed that the deceased man had preferred to walk about the room rather than sleep at night, and had believed that 'people were after him all over the town'. The effects found upon him consisted of a pair of spectacles, some food, and a piece of paper – on which was drawn some rough sketches of saucepans and some writing that could not be deciphered. A verdict of 'found drowned' was returned.

JUNE

Mablethorpe character Eardley 'Hedley' Broddle, *c.* 1905.

The Sad Tale of Jolly Hedley Broddle

Early twentieth-century Mablethorpe character, Eardley 'Hedley' Broddle, was just 4ft tall. Hedley worked for farmer William Codd, trundling his cart around the streets, delivering fresh milk from the churn. To earn a little extra money, he also used to work as a knife cleaner and grinder. Always happy in his employment, he would sing and whistle as he went about his business. His life went full circle and ended rather sadly; he was born in 1846 in Louth and returned in later life, dying there in 1910, aged 64, in the workhouse.

1898   An inquest was held in Spalding upon the body of Robbie Andrew   1 JUNE
(12). The unfortunate lad, an inmate at Spalding Union Workhouse, had been discovered dead when another inmate went to draw some water from the well. The lid was lifted and, even though the opening was just 20in, his body was seen at the bottom of the well. Despite men working within a few yards of the well, no one had seen or heard anything. The boy was known to suffer from fits, and the evidence pointed to him being seized by a convulsion and falling in unconscious. A verdict of 'accidentally drowned' was returned.

1894   Reports were published of an inquest, held at Spalding, touching   2 JUNE
the death of Sally Bott. Sally was an actress who had been on tour in the area with her husband Bates William Bott. The evidence showed that Mrs Bott had received fatal injuries when her dress caught on a chain in the vehicle from which she was alighting, causing her to fall to the ground. The injury was at first thought to be trivial and she had walked some 30 or 40 yards before her lower limbs seemed to fail her. A doctor was called; he arrived five minutes before she died. The medical conclusion was that death was caused by a syncope produced by an internal lesion, probably in the head, caused by the fall. The jury returned a verdict accordingly.

1848   Handbills, distributed across Gainsborough, cautioned publicans   3 JUNE
and others against serving the night watch when the latter ought to be on duty. It was, however, commented in the *Hull Packet*: 'Not one word is said about the police who require a much stronger reprimand, for they are hours in public houses when they ought to be on duty.'

1935   Arthur Barlow (27) of Portland Street, Lincoln, was remanded   4 JUNE
in custody for medical examination, charged with stealing women's clothes from the house where he lodged. Barlow claimed that he had no intention of stealing the garments but had only borrowed them to dress up as a woman. Lincoln Police Chief Constable Hughes commented that, for some time past, Barlow had been a source of anxiety to the police through his mania for appearing in quiet public places dressed in women's clothes; his peculiar behaviour also frightened women and girls. In one incident, a girl was returning from a dance after midnight when she saw a figure in white under a streetlamp. As she approached, the white figure started bowing towards her. The girl believed that she was seeing a ghost and ran in terror for the police. Barlow's mother had previously told the police that the lad had once fallen from a ladder and struck his head, and, since then, the mania for dressing in women's clothes had overtaken him.

1890   Reports were published of the case of Ellen Turner (18), heard   5 JUNE
at Spalding Petty Sessions. Ellen had been in the workhouse for a long

time and had been blind for several years, but was just recovering her sight. She hated her life, claiming that she was not even allowed to sing without being locked up, and resolutely felt that death was preferable to 'being shut up in the workhouse' all her life. One day, she had drawn a cord tightly around her neck and attempted to commit suicide, but had failed and was taken to Lincoln Prison. She said that she was treated kindly in gaol. Ellen went to trial at the South Holland Quarter Sessions and was sentenced to three months' imprisonment for attempted suicide.

6 JUNE **1878** Local eccentric Aaron Dickinson, of Low Toynton Fen near Spilsby, was discovered by PC Dance shortly after midnight, wet and groaning by the side of a drain. He claimed that at about 9 p.m., when approximately 30 yards distant from Miller's Beerhouse, he was set upon by blacksmith Joseph Johnson (26), labourer Charles Stones (25) and boatman George Cooper (29).

With the cry of 'Let's have a game with Old Aaron', Johnson had rushed in front of him, picked up a stone and struck Dickinson on the head with it. Aaron was knocked down, whereupon Johnson and Cooper had taken hold of him by the shoulders and feet and thrown him into the drain, which contained 6ft-deep water. Dickinson had scrambled out, only to be met by Stones and the other men; he had begged not to be ill-treated further. Johnson said that they would 'finish' him this time and threw him into the water twice more.

When brought to court, the defence counsel argued that Dickinson was well known in the district for his eccentric demeanour, and everyone knew that he suffered from hallucinations. The surgeon also examined Aaron thirteen days after the alleged assault, but found no trace of bruises and no trace of an injury to the head, such as would be caused by a blow from a stone. The court was adjourned.

7 JUNE **1858** Thomas Sharp was found asleep during the night by PC No. 8, on the street in Lockhill, Grimsby, in a state of intoxication. When the constable attempted to rouse him, Sharp began to utter abusive language and pulled off his clothes. The constable called for the assistance of another officer and, after considerable difficulty, Sharp was brought to the lock-up. Police Constable No. 3 corroborated this. He had to remain several hours with the prisoner to prevent him from laying violent hands upon himself. When Sharp was brought into court he was in a state bordering upon nudity, having torn his upper garments into tatters. He was charged with assaulting PC No. 8 while in the execution of his duty. In his defence, Sharp claimed that he had not assaulted the officers, at least not to any extent. He also said that he could not see how a little fellow like him could do anything in the way of resistance to two policemen, and, as for destroying his clothes, that was done by the arresting officers and not by him. Their Worships told him they had no doubt that he had a purpose in destroying his clothes (to get a new set at the expense of the local authorities), and the superintendent reported that he was a returned convict, having been transported for a robbery at Cleethorpes. The prisoner, who had a most impudent leer on his countenance, was committed to the House of Correction for a month on each charge, with hard labour.

John Howard Reports on the Prisons of Lincolnshire: 8 JUNE

Spalding Bridewell [visited 1776]. This prison, lately built, has several sizeable airy rooms thirteen by ten: chimneys in some of them. A work-room twenty-eight feet by nine and three quarters. The under-rooms vaulted, twelve feet and a half by nine and a half. No yard: no water accessible to prisoners. When they work they have three fourths of the profit; Turnkey has the remainder. Clauses of Act against Spirituous Liquors hung up as also is the late Act of Preserving the Health of Prisoners, neatly painted on a small board. Keeper's salary £38: Fees 5s. no Table. Keeper told me that in the last six years he had 236 prisoners.

1854 The findings from the Crowland murder inquest were published. 9 JUNE According to witness statements, Joseph Baines (38) had been seen entering the home of his father-in-law, Farmer Hickling, on South Street. A few minutes later, Mrs Sarah Hickling had rushed out screaming 'Murder', followed by Baines with a poker in his hand. A few yards from the door, Sarah had fallen to the ground and was subject to a hail of blows from the poker, which was wielded by Baines. By the time Mr Ringrose, the shoemaker, had come running and intervened, Mrs Hickling was unconscious; Baines had then dropped the poker and fled. Ringrose said that he had been afraid to seize Baines because he 'looked very wild' and he feared for his own safety. Suddenly Baines had returned and dealt Mrs Hickling another blow, before taking to his heels.

The post-mortem revealed that her skull was fractured from ear to ear, with several portions of her shattered skull driven into her brain. It took a number of constables to catch and restrain Baines and get him into custody, where he started complaining, 'Oh, my poor mind!' and began walking around the room where he was held, complaining that the air was 'oppressive'. The inquest returned a verdict of 'wilful murder' against Baines and he was sent for trial at the Lincoln Assizes, where he was acquitted of the murder on the grounds of insanity.

1821 A storm of hail and thunder, lightning and rain occurred at 10 JUNE Carlby. It was so severe that the afternoon service was delayed by order of the minister; this was most fortunate, for an enormous ball of electric fire, accompanied with a tremendous explosion, fell into the steeple of the church, set the rafters in flames, melted the lead, drove down part of a wall and did other serious damage.

11 JUNE 1832 A group of young men committed a burglary in the house of Miss Sarah Dixon at Merton. Entering through a window, they were heard by Miss Dixon, who raised the alarm by ringing a bell out of another window. The men rapidly decamped, taking two brass candlesticks and an extinguisher with them. They were all soon in custody; one of their number, a man named Weston, having turned King's Evidence. Thomas Leedham (17), Harrison Cawdell (17), Joseph Marsh (24) and Thomas Ford (20) were found guilty and sentenced to death. This was commuted to transportation for life. William Marsh (25) was charged with – in the company of some of those aforementioned – breaking into the premises of George Naylor at Gainsborough and stealing a box containing clothes. He was also found guilty and sentenced to death, later commuted to transportation for fourteen years.

12 JUNE 1890 William Pritchard, a night watchman at HMP Lincoln, was brought before the justices charged with stealing four flower pots, thirteen roots and cut flowers to the value of 1s 6d from his employers, the Prison Commissioners. It transpired that Pritchard had been employed as a watchman for nine years. He had been on duty outside the gaol on the night of 1/2 June; the following morning, Chief Warder Grisdale and Warder Keyworth had found the aforementioned items, along with a counterfeit key to the prison garden, in Pritchard's basket. Pritchard pleaded guilty and was sentenced to three months' imprisonment.

13 JUNE Cures of Cunning Folk in Fen and Wold: Cramp
Folks once tried to prevent cramp by wearing a ring of gold coffin handles; a 'crampe ringe', blessed by the reigning sovereign, was considered especially efficacious. For less affluent people, a quick word with a 'cunning woman' would probably result in the advice to place one's boots or shoes by the bedside in the form of a 'cross tau'. They might also have been told to place a periwinkle under the mattress. Another preventative charm for cramp was to obtain the knee-bone of a sheep, a coffin handle or a human patella from the local sexton (the latter was considered the most potent). The object was to be carried in a pocket, the nearer the skin the better, or placed under the pillow at night.

14 JUNE 1864 An inquest was held in Brigg upon the body of William Walker (74), a farm labourer. Walker had been an inmate at Brigg Workhouse for two or three months before finding work in Broughton. However, he had faced a return to the workhouse when his employment was terminated. After telling his wife, who lived in Brigg, that he was returning, he had called in at Brown's Chemist and bought an ounce of laudanum, saying it was for his sore feet. He had stayed at a Brigg lodging house and was discovered, dying, the following morning. Dr Daunt was summoned and

A Lincolnshire sexton – just the man to see if you suffer from cramp.

attempted to treat Walker, but the unfortunate man died shortly after. A bottle containing only a few drops of laudanum was found in his pocket. The jury returned a verdict of 'death from an overdose of laudanum, inadvertently administered by the deceased himself'.

15 JUNE **1858** The case of Marshall Higgins, a native of the Emerald Isle, was reported. He was charged with being drunk and disorderly, and with assaulting the police while being apprehended and after he was taken to the lock-up. Higgins complained that he had had a disgusting epithet applied to him and, feeling his native pride touched, and further fired up by drink, he had lashed out. Despite losing all command over himself, he did not think he should have been abused in the manner that he was by the police, who had swollen his arm very much by the use of their batons. The evidence of the police went to show that the conduct of the prisoner was extremely violent and that he had repeatedly kicked at and struck them. Their Worships remarked that the policemen must stand in their own defence when attacked, and sentenced Higgins to pay a fine of 5 guineas and 9s expenses before the evening, or go to the House of Correction for a month.

16 JUNE **Punishments of the Past: The Scold's Bridle**
The bane of Early Modern British life was the scold, nagging wife, rumourmonger or malicious village gossip. The

judiciary, with its usual robust approach to such social problems, devised the scold's bridle. There were several different designs but the basic construction consisted of a lockable iron framework in the form of a helmet-shaped cage that fitted tightly over the head. An aperture was provided for the mouth, and a small, flat metal plate protruded into the unfortunate woman's mouth when the bridle was worn, to hold her tongue down or prevent speech – hence the term 'Hold your tongue!' Such devices are known to have been in use across the country until the late eighteenth century.

The scold's bridle.

17 JUNE **1814** The case of two youths, named King and Richards, was reported. The boys had climbed the steeple of All Saints' Church in Stamford. The ascent had taken about twelve minutes and was achieved by means of crockets, or projecting stones, on the outside of the spire – twenty-six in number, 3ft asunder – as the bell was ringing. After Richards had hung his waistcoat on the weathercock, the pair had descended safely again. The waistcoat remained on the weathercock for some time afterwards, as a memento of the feat.

18 JUNE **1884** The case of John Green was reported. Green had been angling in the River Witham, at Lincoln, when he had suddenly dragged the body of a man to the surface. The deceased was later identified as James Connor (34), a prisoner recently released from Lincoln County Prison.

All Saints' Church,
Stamford, *c.* 1905.

High Bridge and
Glory Hole, Lincoln,
c. 1910.

It transpired that Connor had gone out for a drink to celebrate his release, had got drunk and was thought to have fallen in the river as a result of being intoxicated. A verdict of 'found drowned' was returned.

19 JUNE   **1857**   The case of Elizabeth Ashton was reported. Elizabeth had been suffering with 'depression of spirits' as a result of ill-health and weakness, and had complained of feeling a great pain in her head after a shutter had fallen on her. She was reported missing from her home in Maiden Row, Louth and was later discovered, fearfully disfigured, after floating in the waters of the River Lud for eight days. The inquest jury returned a verdict of 'found drowned'.

20 JUNE   **1888**   As the Great Eastern express from Cambridge to Doncaster was leaving Spalding railway station, Thomas Allen, the driver, ascended the tender for some purpose. The train continued to move and Allen's head came into violent contact with the ironwork of a bridge; Allen was knocked to the ground and, when he was picked up, he was found to be dead.

21 JUNE   **1854**   A case was reported concerning the porters of the Manchester, Sheffield & Lincolnshire Railway at Grimsby, who were transferring goods from a London train when they discovered a package marked 'glass, with care' addressed to a reverend gentleman in a nearby village.

The parcel aroused suspicion; it was consequently opened and found to contain the body of the daughter of this man. It was parcelled up again and sent to its destination – with a bill of extra charges for carrying a corpse. As a case of merchandise, the parcel would have cost £1 4s but, being what it was, the charge was £8.

1855 On this day, an inquest was held at the Plough in Upgate, Louth, upon the body of James Storer Brooks, an agricultural servant. A fortnight previously, he had been driving a wagon and team of horses on the London Road. He had attempted to leap from the shafts but had fallen – and the wheels had passed over both legs, fracturing the thigh on one and the ankle on the other. The injuries proved to be severe and 'he sank under them'. The verdict returned was 'accidental death'. **22 JUNE**

1855 The case of George 'Doggy' Parker was reported. This well-known disorderly character was brought before the magistrates charged by his sister, Fanny Horsewood, with assaulting and wounding her with a cleaver. It was stated that Parker had gone to his parents' house 'in a furious state of intoxication' and a quarrel had arisen. He had dashed out a window, demolished several articles of furniture and, when remonstrated with, had grabbed a butcher's cleaver and an axe with which he commenced an indiscriminate attack upon the family. He was remanded but, having attested to serve in the Grenadier Guards, his sister withdrew the charge against him. **23 JUNE**

Strange Tales and Folklore of Lincolnshire: Funeral Customs for Women and Men. **24 JUNE**
Ethel Rudkin recorded the following in *Lincolnshire Folklore* (1936):

> At village funerals it used to be the custom for a woman to be carried by women [all maids if she was a maid] ... White towels were put under the coffin to carry it by, in the case of a woman's funeral and the women who 'carried' wore a long skirt hanging about a foot below the dress and over the head a piece of white calico was worn, that was drawn together at the back – the ends came down under the neck and were tied beneath the chin in a white bow, this looked something like a nun's head dress and they wore white gloves.

The custom for a man was to be carried by male pallbearers:

> ...when men 'carried' [the coffin] the men wore bowler hats with a white cloth like a towel tied around and the ends hanging down behind.

There would be four or six bearers, depending on the distance that they had to walk. No matter what the sex of the deceased, in Lincolnshire past, one rule was applied above all – never forget to tie the feet. This

St Mary's
churchyard,
Marshchapel.

was done to prevent the corpse's return, or in case some other spirit took possession of the body for its own purposes; with the legs tied, they would be going nowhere.

25 JUNE **Punishments of the Past: Broad Arrow Men**

A common term applied to convicts in the late nineteenth and early twentieth centuries was 'broad arrow men', an epithet gained from the distinctive broad arrow or 'crow's foot' mark which was stamped onto all prison uniforms. The origins of the symbol date back to the seventeenth century, when a Master of the Ordnances in the Tower of London began marking the weaponry as Tower property with an arrow-like device from his coat of arms. Over the years, this symbol

Prisoner C406, Lucas, J. A young broad arrow man, November 1904.

has been adopted by all government departments, to denote equipment as diverse as military vehicle parts and rifles to rulers and paperweights as Government Issue. The broad arrow was stamped onto prison garb not only to create a 'dress of shame' to be worn by convicts, but also to make the clothes they wore so distinctive that they would stand out as a convict if they effected an escape. Broad arrow symbols were discontinued on prison uniforms in 1922.

26 JUNE **1832**   The following toll was published for Gainsborough during the cholera epidemic:

	New Cases	Dead	Recovered	Remaining
June 14	5	2	0	7
June 15	1	0	1	7
June 16	2	2	1	6
June 17	9	2	4	9
June 19	2	1	0	10
June 20	1	1	5	5

The situation appeared to be improving in Gainsborough. It was hoped that early attention to bowel disorders (the general premonitory stage in this fearful disease), which was strongly recommended by the medical gentleman of the town, had produced its proper effect. However, cholera had spread as far away as Manchester and Stockport.

27 JUNE **1777**   Anglican clergyman, Dr William Dodd, was executed in Tyburn, London, on this day. Born the son of the rector of Bourne on 29 May 1729, he left home aged 16 to attend Clare Hall in Cambridge and was ordained a priest in 1753. Dodd showed great promise; he obtained a number of parishes in London, and attained high honours – such as being made Chaplain in Ordinary to George III in 1763 and a Doctor of Laws at Cambridge in 1766. He wrote a novel, a number of theological

Dr Dodd composing his *Thoughts in Prison* while in the condemned cell at Newgate.

tracts, a commentary on the Bible and, probably his most famous work, *The Beauties of Shakespeare* (1752). Dodd appeared to attract fame and fortune; his wife even won £1,000 in a lottery, a fantastic sum in its day.

The problem was that Dodd enjoyed the high life to such a degree that he became known as 'The Macaroni Parson' (macaroni was a derogatory term for the more outlandish and epicene dandies) and, despite all his good fortune, his finances were often in a precarious state. After a risible attempt at bribery to secure a lucrative position, he was reduced to making a clumsy forgery to clear his debts. Clearly the act of a desperate man, he forged a bond for the sum of £4,200 in the name of his patron, the Earl of Chesterfield. The bond was accepted by the bank on good faith, but a blot on the signature caused the bank to write to his lordship to request a new, clean copy. Upon receipt of the paperwork from his bank, the forgery was rapidly detected by Chesterfield. Dodd immediately confessed and begged for a chance to make amends – but he was thrown into Wood Street Compter (a small prison) to await his trial. Tried at the Old Bailey, Dodd was found guilty of the forgery and sentenced to death. There was a public outcry – some 23,000 people gave their names to a petition for his pardon – and even the eminent Dr Johnson wrote several papers in defence of Dodd, all to no avail. Dodd spent his time between condemnation and the gallows at Newgate, writing his last book, a blank verse entitled *Thoughts in Prison*. What was claimed to be Dodd's *The Convict's Address to his Unhappy Brethren* was, in fact, mostly written by Samuel Johnson who, when quizzed about the authorship of the piece, 'defended' Dodd by stating: 'When a man knows he is to be hanged in a fortnight, it concentrates his mind wonderfully.'

1703   John Wesley, the man who was to become the founder of the   **28 JUNE**
Methodist Church, was born in Epworth.

In December 1716, a servant of the Wesleys answered a knock at the door to find no one there. He blamed youngsters' high jinks but, later that day, he saw a corn-grinding hand mill turning without human help and so began to wonder what was going on. Strange events began to be an everyday occurrence in the Wesleys' parsonage. At 9.45 each evening, the family heard the heavy steps of a man coming down the stairs in the north-east corner of the house, but no one was there. They gave the 'spirit' the name of 'Old Jeffrey'. The poltergeist activity intensified. In one instance, John's parents, Samuel and Susanna, were descending the stairs and heard a noise which sounded like someone was emptying a large bag of coins at their feet. This was followed by the sound of glass bottles being 'dashed to a thousand pieces'. Other sounds heard were running footsteps, groans, and a door latch being lifted several times. After two months, Wesley's father Samuel was determined not to share his house with a spirit; indeed, he had become convinced that it was an agent of evil sent to test their faith, so he

John Wesley of
Epworth, founder
of the Methodist
Church.

challenged the spirit to meet him alone in the study. Samuel entered
the room, only to have a powerful force push the door in his face.
He struggled through and demanded that the spirit identify itself.
His questions were answered by furious knocking from each wall in
turn, which built to a terrifying crescendo. Parson Wesley remained
indomitable and the spirit's anger and power appeared to subside, until
it faded away and the house was left in peace once more.

29 JUNE   1885   The following incident was reported on this day. A servant
of Sir W.E. Welby-Gregory of Denton Manor, near Grantham, was
experimenting with a new fire escape and threw herself down, intending
to show everybody present how an escape could be made. She fell a
distance of about 40ft and sustained a serious injury to the spine.

30 JUNE   **Punishments of the Past: The Treadwheel**
The treadwheel was devised in the early nineteenth century by Norfolk-
born engineer William Cubitt. The principle of the treadwheel was simple.

Looking like an elongated mill wheel, each wheel contained twenty-four steps set 8in apart, so the circumference of the cylinder was 16ft. The wheel, under the power of the convicts walking up its 'steps', revolved twice in a minute; a mechanism was set to ring a bell on every thirtieth revolution, to announce that the spell of work had finished. Every man put to labour at the wheel worked fifteen quarter-hour sessions, climbing up to 18,000ft every day. The number of prisoners usually employed at this labour was between twelve and twenty. There were also capstans to push around for those unable to walk the treadmill. Both of these devices were connected to pumps, which supplied water for the use of prisoners and cleansed their sewers. In 1895, there were thirty-nine treadwheels and twenty-nine cranks in use in British prisons. Treadwheels were finally banned by an Act of Parliament in 1898.

Prisoners stepping the treadwheel.

JULY

Oliver Cromwell.

The Battle of Gainsborough

On 20 July 1643, Lord Willoughby captured Gainsborough for Parliament. Threatened by a detachment of Royalist cavalry (commanded by Sir Charles Cavendish), Sir John Meldrum and Colonel Oliver Cromwell were despatched as reinforcements. They were joined by a body of local troops at North Scarle and marched to Gainsborough. On 28 July, the Parliamentarian reinforcements encountered Cavendish's advance guard of dragoons to the south of Gainsborough. The main body of Royalists was positioned on top of Foxby Hill. The Parliamentarians drove the Royalist dragoons back and decimated the main body of the Royalists in a furious cavalry charge. Cromwell realised that Cavendish had kept his own regiment in reserve and was preparing a counterattack. Rallying his troopers, Cromwell allowed Cavendish's force to ride past, then led a charge against the Royalist rear. Cavendish was killed in the mêlée and the Royalists retreated. Later that day, the Royalist Earl of Newcastle's main northern army advanced to besiege Gainsborough. The Parliamentarians knew when to quit and retreated to Boston, with Cromwell's troopers fighting a disciplined rearguard action, covering the withdrawal of the infantry. After successfully taking Lincoln, Newcastle left to besiege Hull, leaving some of his army in Lincolnshire. In his absence, they were defeated at Winceby by Cromwell on 11 October 1643, a battle that led to the loss of the whole county to Parliament.

Strange Tales and Folklore of Lincolnshire: The Lincolnshire Giantess

Ann Hardy, known as the 'Rippingale Giantess' or the 'Lincolnshire Giantess', died in July 1815, aged 16. The daughter of Thomas and Sarah Hardy – people of no special height – she stood 6ft 1in tall by the age of 13 and was described as 'well proportioned'. She had attracted much attention in the county after being exhibited at fairs as 'a phenomenon'. Ann eventually stood at 7ft 2in and, at the time of her death, was the tallest woman in Britain. Her coffin measured a length of 7ft ½in, and 2ft 7in across the shoulders. Ann lies in an unmarked grave in Rippingale churchyard.

Rippingale church and churchyard, the resting place of Ann Hardy, 'The Lincolnshire Giantess'.

2 JULY 1858   On this day, newspapers reported the tragic story of a young girl named Lingard. After two years together, the man she loved had married another woman on the very day upon which Lingard had expected to become his bride. The blow was so cruel and unexpected that she rapidly declined, and in six weeks she was dead – her physician said 'from a broken heart'.

3 JULY John Howard Reports on the Prisons of Lincolnshire:

Stamford Town Gaol [visited 1776]. The Gate which was the old prison and Town-Hall is taken down. The only room now made use of is in the Gaoler's house which joined to the gate. There is a new prison building behind the new Town-Hall. The part of it that is finished has two cells, about twelve feet by eight: the window in each only two feet by four inches and a half. The Bridewell room is sixteen feet by eight feet three inches: the window here is also too small, two feet by one foot eight inches. Allowance to Felons two pence a day. Salary as Gaoler £4: Salary as Keeper £3 6s 8d.

John Howard, prison reformer.

4 JULY 1829   Joseph Neal Sewell, the man commonly known as the 'Lincolnshire Giant', died. While alive, he was 7ft 4ins tall and weighed 37 stone. Sewell had required 5 yards of broadcloth for his coat, 5 yards of lining for his waistcoat and 7 yards of patent cord for his trousers. His shoes were 14.5in long and 6.5in wide.

Sewell, who was born at Scamblesby near Horncastle on 18 February 1805, was an illegitimate child. Consequently, he was soon compelled to seek his own livelihood and, as he was remarkably large for his age, he began making a living as a public curiosity. At 14, weighing 20 stone, he was exhibited as a 'fat boy'. About three years prior to his death, he was seized with a typhus fever while visiting Swansea; this fever resulted in blindness, and he was reduced to going into the poorhouse. On recovering from his illness, he proceeded through the country – blind, feeble, and almost helpless. When he reached Bristol, his melancholy condition attracted the attention of some benevolent persons, who liberally administered to his necessities, and eventually enabled him to proceed to Exeter, where he was furnished with a caravan in which to exhibit himself and provided with an attendant named Broomsgrove. Thus supplied, Sewell became tolerably successful and again reached Swansea. His state of health, although weak, did not indicate any proximate danger. However, after taking tea on 3 July he was seized with fits, of which he died the next day, aged 24.

Sewell had been horrified by the idea of anatomical operations after death, and his friends, in deference to his wish, refused many lucrative offers for his body. A Somersetshire dwarf named Farnham, who stood 37in high, followed the caravan as chief mourner at the funeral. The contrasting stature of this individual, with that of Sewell, had presented a curious spectacle when the latter was alive, and had rendered the conjoint exhibition exceedingly attractive to spectators. The funeral drew a vast concourse of the inhabitants at it passed through the streets of Taunton, and Sewell was buried in the churchyard of St Mary Magdalene. Quicklime was thrown into the grave (to speed up decomposition) and the best expedients were adopted to accomplish the wishes of the deceased, regarding the security of his remains from bodysnatchers.

5 JULY **1878** At the Lincolnshire Quarter Sessions, held at Lincoln Castle, comment was made upon the numerous cases of sheep stealing in the county. Something had to be done, so an example was made of two men. A tailor named Thomas Codd had been found guilty of stealing ewes and five lambs from two farms near Market Rasen. In a separate case, Edward Rands had stolen five sheep and five lambs from Mr James Johnson at Holton; he had then attacked PC Toyne when the policeman had queried his possession of the sheep as he left the scene. Both Codd and Rands were sent down, with five years' penal servitude each.

6 JULY **1895** Sarah Gibson (15) was brought before Lincolnshire Assizes indicted for the murder of her brother, John Henry Gibson, at Asterby. Sarah lived at home with her parents and two siblings, and had been described as being of 'weak intellect' since birth. On 6 April 1895, Sarah had been left in charge of her infant brother while her mother popped out to a neighbouring village. When Sarah's father, farm labourer William Gibson, had returned, he found that Sarah was not in the house and 2-year-old John was lying in a pool of blood on the hearth rug. When arrested, Sarah said that she had hit little Johnnie on the head with a poker 'because she was mad with him' for pushing her. At the Assizes, Dr J.W. Marsh, Medical Superintendent of the Bracebridge Lunatic Asylum, was called as a witness. He had examined the prisoner and was of the opinion that she was incapable of understanding the nature of the proceedings and was not capable of pleading. Dr Brook, Deputy Medical Officer of Lincoln Prison, who had also kept Sarah under observation, concurred with Dr Marsh. The jury returned a verdict to the effect that Sarah was insane, and she was detained at Her Majesty's pleasure.

7 JULY **1879** Charlotte Wallis, a shopkeeper from Waterside North, was brought before Lincoln Police Court, charged with unlawfully causing George Steels to convey tobacco into HMP Lincoln. Steels was likewise charged with attempting to introduce tobacco into the prison. The evidence revealed that Wallis had got Steels to carry a dinner into the gaol, intended for a man named Thomas Wells, a prisoner awaiting trial. When Warder Keyworth had examined the food before it was given to the prisoner, he had found a quantity of tobacco sandwiched between two pieces of bread. Steels was taken before Major Mackay, the Governor of the prison, and was questioned; he claimed that he was not aware of the contents. Tracing the dinner back to Wallis, she freely admitted to Detective Parlby that Steels had no knowledge of the contents. In court, Wallis claimed that she had not thought she was breaking the law. Found guilty, she was sentenced to six months' imprisonment or a fine of £20. However, because this was the first case of its kind that the Governor had heard of, the penalty was reduced to 20s or fourteen days' imprisonment in default. Steels was discharged.

8 JULY   **1854**   A young man named Biggadike and two friends were driving through Fleet in a cart. As they trotted along, the lash of Biggadike's whip became entangled in a portion of the harness. He pulled it out with such a violent jerk that the end of it flew back and cut him severely over the eye, forcing the eyeball out of the socket so that it hung down upon his cheek. He was immediately taken to the Bull Inn. The party then returned to Holbeach, where, at the time the report was written, Biggadike remained 'in a precarious state'.

9 JULY   **1892**   Between 11 p.m. and midnight, railway labourer Robert Wright and a number of other young men were returning from a political meeting when, as they passed PC Edward Woods, one of them called him 'bright buttons'. PC Woods grabbed a lad called Pearson. Wright remonstrated with the policeman, saying that Pearson was not the one who had called him the name. Woods retorted, 'You -------, you can have it if you want it,' then struck Wright in the chest, knocked him down, and struck at him again when he was on the floor. The incident was brought before Spalding Sessions and PC Woods was fined £20.

10 JULY   **Cures of Cunning Folk in Fen and Wold: To Avoid Pregnancy**
To avoid an unwanted pregnancy, it was once suggested that the unfortunate girl held a dead man's hand for two minutes. This was believed to

A corpse in its shroud.

be so efficacious that the girl would be 'immunised' against fertilisation for two years! Soaking pennies from the church collection in vinegar, then applying the vinegar to the woman's most intimate parts, was seen as another safeguard.

1893   Christopher Barker (60), a Lincoln joiner known for his 'eccentric   **11 JULY** and singular character', was due to appear before local magistrates on a charge of using abusive language against his Danesgate neighbours, Lucy Jane Wilkinson and her 'lodger' Crosha James Creasey (28), an assistant master at a Wesleyan day school. Creasey had formerly lodged with Barker and had entered into an affair with Barker's niece, who lived with him at the time. Creasey had then left the niece for their next-door neighbour, Lucy Wilkinson. Barker bore a grudge and had shouted verbal abuse at both Wilkinson and Creasey on a number of occasions.

Barker was due in court at 10 a.m. on 11 July. However, at 8 a.m. he went to the palings between his home and the house where Wilkinson lived and Creasey lodged. Wilkinson was in the garden cleaning boots. Barker asked her if he could see Creasey, but Wilkinson said she would not allow him to enter her house. Barker replied, 'You won't?' and jumped over the railings. Wilkinson ran to get inside her house but Barker caught her in the doorway, put his arm around her neck, fired his revolver in her face and allowed her to drop to the floor. Barker then stepped over her body and found Creasey, shooting him in the head while he was shaving. The police arrived and found that Barker had locked himself inside his own house, next door to the scene of crime. He appeared at a downstairs window with the revolver, which he put in his mouth but did not fire. While some police officers distracted him in conversation, two others crept in the back, but only managed to seize and secure Barker after a desperate struggle. Fortunately, Wilkinson had only been wounded in her left cheek; Creasey was dead.

At Barker's trial for murder before the County Assizes, questions over his sanity were raised but Barker was found guilty and sentenced to death. Subsequently, he was examined by two experts on insanity; one from Woking, the other from Broadmoor Criminal Lunatic Asylum. Advice was given to the Secretary of State and Barker's sentence was commuted to penal servitude for life.

1955   The last man to hang in Lincolnshire was executed on this day.   **12 JULY** Kenneth Roberts (24) was married and living in Scunthorpe, where he worked as a warehouseman. He was found guilty of murdering Mary Georgina Roberts (18) – no relation to the accused – by strangling her with a scarf in a wood yard off the Winterton Road in Scunthorpe. He had telephoned the police himself and confessed that he had just 'gone crazy'. Found guilty of murder, he was executed by Doncaster hangman, Steve Wade.

13 JULY 1889 The Lincoln coroner held an inquest upon the body of John Edward Hill, a young man who, while bathing in the shallow part of a river with some friends, had ducked under. In doing so, his body had caught against an old coal scuttle at the bottom of the water, which tore open his abdomen to such an extent that his bowels protruded. Removed to hospital, another wound was found in his large intestine and all hopes of his recovery were abandoned. The poor fellow lingered for three days then finally expired. A verdict of 'accidental death' was returned.

14 JULY 1896 The death of Joseph Charles Edwards (82) was reported. Edwards had been the rector of Ingoldmells for the previous thirty-two years. Despite having both literary and musical talents, the newspapers commented about him: 'No inconsiderable portion of the time, he has spent in Lincoln Prison for debtors "laying out" unsatisfied judgements.' He had been chronically bankrupt for years and, having no other living relative, had obtained money by sending begging letters. Indeed, he had perfected this skill until it almost became a fine art to him – the *Daily Telegraph* commented that Edwards was 'the most notorious begging letter writer in the Church of England'.

15 JULY 1864 PC William Antcliffe had been on duty in the Lindsey division until 3 p.m. before returning to his lodgings in South Carlton. On entering the house, he complained of suffering from a severe toothache and, knowing that laudanum was kept in the house for sheep dressing, he asked for a little to relieve the pain. His landlady handed him a bottle containing about 2 or 3 ounces, which he took in her presence. She then carefully locked the rest up in a drawer. Immediately after her departure, Antcliffe bolted the door, forced open the drawer and swallowed the rest of the contents. When the landlady returned she tried the door but, finding it fastened, she looked through the window – where she saw Antcliffe lying on the bed 'kicking'. The door was broken open and medical assistance was obtained. The doctor tried to help but Antcliffe declared that, if he survived, he would only cut his throat. He was removed to Lincoln County Hospital, where he died upon arrival. No cause could be found for Antcliffe's rash actions. A verdict of 'suicide' was returned.

16 JULY 1894 An inquest was held at Mablethorpe concerning the death of Alfred Larder (35), a visitor from Leeds who was born at Louth. His body had been discovered by Charles Slack, another visitor from Sheffield, who had seen a man sitting on the sand hills at Mablethorpe, apparently asleep but with a revolver in his right hand. Slack had called for assistance and, as they approached the body, they had spotted a bullet wound in the forehead. At the inquest, it was revealed that the deceased had formerly lived with his wife and child in Leeds. It was rather cruelly stated that, 'beyond publishing a few novels [he] had done nothing for the last ten years', and had left his wife without any means. PC Windley confirmed that Larder had not had any money in his pockets, but there was a letter addressed to the coroner. It contained reflections upon certain individuals, whom he claimed:

> ... have robbed me, ruined me, broken my heart and driven me to kill myself. This may sound strange language, but a dying man does not lie. If I am allowed to return to earth, they will have a choking in the throat, for I shall haunt them.

The jury returned a verdict of 'suicide during a fit of temporary insanity'.

Mablethorpe High Street, *c.* 1910.

17 JULY

1889 Around noon, an elderly carter named Porter, employed by F. Ward of Quarrington, was proceeding down a hill in Folkingham on a horse and dray which was loaded with iron. The hill had a steep incline and the horse was travelling at a furious rate. Suddenly, Mr Porter was pitched out of the vehicle and the wheels passed over him, crushing his head. He was conveyed to a doctor in Sleaford but there was little hope of recovery.

18 JULY

1777 Henry Atkinson was executed at Lincoln for the murder of his baby. Atkinson claimed that he had been unaware of his wife's pregnancy when he married her, and was not convinced the baby was even his. He had vented his wrath by crushing the head of the babe with his knees. Named as the culprit at the inquest, Atkinson was tried at the Assizes, found guilty and was hanged six days later.

19 JULY

1847 Reuben Thacker was brought before Lincolnshire Assizes, charged with stealing items of wearing apparel, plus six ewes and twelve calves, which were the property of John Ewinson, at Barrowby. Thacker was arrested while en route to delivering his stolen animals, when he stopped off for the night at the Plough Inn, Wilsford. Thacker admitted to driving the sheep but not to the theft. He was found guilty on both charges and sentenced to four months' imprisonment with hard labour for the theft of the clothes, followed by seven years' transportation for stealing the sheep.

20 JULY   **1722**   On this day, Eleanor Elsom was burnt to death, at Lincoln, for the murder of her husband. On the day of her execution, Eleanor was dressed in a cloth 'made like a shift' which was saturated with tar; her limbs were smeared likewise and a tar bonnet was placed upon her head. She was brought out of the prison barefoot and placed upon a hurdle, which was drawn upon a sledge to the place of execution, near the gallows. Upon arrival, some time was passed in prayer, after which the executioner placed her upon a 3ft-tar barrel against the stake. A rope ran through a pulley in the stake and was placed around her neck; she herself fixed it there. Three irons also held her body to the stake, and the rope was pulled tight; the tar barrel was taken aside and the fire was lit. It was believed that she died before the flames reached her, as the executioner had pulled on the rope several times while the irons were being fixed. The dryness of the wood and the quantity of tar saw to it that the fire was exceedingly fierce; the body could be seen among the flames for some half an hour before it was fully consumed.

Burning at the stake – the horrific penalty for petty treason.

1809   Daniel Lambert, one of the biggest men of his age, died on this day. Lambert was born in Leicester, the son of the keeper of the county bridewell. As a youth, he was robust but nimble, a keen sportsman and a good swimmer. He ate regularly but frugally and his intake of ale was minimal. At the age of 21, he followed his father to become the keeper of the bridewell – and it was then that Lambert began to gain weight rapidly.

Within two years, by 1793, Lambert's weight was 32 stone. In 1804 his weight increased to over 49 stone. Apparently, his enlarged physique did not interfere with his ability to keep the bridewell, and he was well thought of by magistrates and inmates alike. Lambert was active and bred fighting cocks and dogs, such as setters and pointers and his beloved greyhounds. In 1804, the bridewell closed and Lambert was granted a pension.

In 1806, Lambert conceived the idea of exhibiting himself for profit. To enable this, he commissioned a special carriage to take him to London, where he charged 5s a head for people to view him. He then entered into a grand tour of the country and managed to earn a good living from it.

In June 1809, Lambert arrived in Stamford for the races. He lodged at the Wagon & Horses Inn in St Martins and died there suddenly, aged

Daniel Lambert.

just 39 years old, on Wednesday 21 June. At the time of his death, he stood at a height of 5ft 11in; his waist was 9ft 4in; his calves measured 3ft 1in at their widest; and he weighed a massive 52 stone 11lbs. There was no post-mortem and he was buried two days later, though 'his remains had been kept quite as long as was prudent'. His body was taken out of the ground-floor apartments in which he had been accommodated (he had long been incapable of ascending a staircase) by removing the window and part of the wall to make a passage for the coffin.

Lambert's coffin contained 112 superficial feet of elm; it was 6ft 4in long, 4ft 4in wide, and 2ft 4in deep; his immense legs made it necessary for the coffin to be made in the form of a square case. It was built upon two axle-trees and four clog-wheels, and upon these the remains of the great man were rolled into his grave in the new burial ground at St Martins. A regular descent was made to the grave by cutting away the earth for some distance. A vast multitude of people followed the remains to the grave; the most perfect decorum was preserved and not the slightest accident occurred. A headstone and footstone were erected later by Daniel's friends in Leicester.

22 JULY   1796   Edward Coxon, a deserter from the South Lincolnshire Militia, was hanged at Lincoln. After deserting, Coxon had joined forces with

The end of Edward Coxon.

William Holmes and they had become highway robbers. Their downfall came when they set upon Bourne butcher, Edwin Clarke, who had been travelling home from Stamford races in June 1796. He had run off and Coxon had fired at him, missing his target. A 'Hue and Cry' was raised and eventually Coxon and Holmes were tracked down and arrested. Brought before the Summer Assizes, both were sentenced to death. Holmes was reprieved but, because he had fired the pistol, Coxon went to the gallows.

23 JULY   1801   On this day, Susannah Mottershall was executed for the murder of farmer Samuel Glew of Epworth. Elizabeth Lamb (26) and Susannah Mottershall, alias Mottershed (23), were accused of attacking Glew with an axe, robbing him of property to the value of £40, and throwing his body into a ditch. When brought before the Assizes at Lincoln, Lamb admitted King's Evidence and Mottershall was found guilty, whereupon the sentence of death was pronounced. She was hanged in front of a large crowd at noon. Contemporary accounts recorded that 'The unfortunate woman met her melancholy fate with becoming fortitude ... her body was afterwards delivered to the surgeons for dissection.'

24 JULY   1909   John George Haigh, the 'Acid Bath Murderer', was born at Stamford in Lincolnshire on this day. The son of John and Emily Haigh, he grew up in a Plymouth Brethren household and was a bright lad, winning a scholarship to the Grammar School and Wakefield Cathedral, where he became a choirboy. Sadly, Haigh grew into a man who wanted to live the high life of a gentleman, with hotel accommodation, flash cars and club ties – but he simply did not have the money, and decided he could 'get rich quick' by a fraud, which landed him in prison.

Next he tried murder for gain. His first victims, the McSwans, were all killed in Gloucester Road in London. He then placed them in 40-gallon drums filled with sulphuric acid; this soon dissolved their bodies to sludge, which he disposed of down the drain. Haigh stole the McSwans' pensions, cheques and even sold their properties. He raised himself thousands of pounds and moved into the Onslow Court Hotel in Kensington. The problem was that Haigh was a gambler, and this, combined with his expensive lifestyle, meant that he was soon running short of money – so he found another couple to kill and rob.

On 12 February 1948, Haigh lured Dr Archibald Henderson and his wife, Rose, to his small workshop in Leopold Road, Crawley, West Sussex. When each arrived, Haigh shot them in the head and disposed of their bodies in drums of acid. His final victim was Mrs Olive Durand-Deacon,

John Haigh, 'The Acid Bath Murderer'. (Courtesy of Stewart P. Evans)

who resided, like Haigh, at the Onslow Court Hotel. Haigh took her to his workshop and sent her the same way as the others. Mrs Durand-Deacon had a friend who was very suspicious about what had happened to her, and reported Olive missing to the police, mentioning her acquaintance with Haigh. The police looked into Haigh's background and his criminal record; a search of his workshop revealed Mrs Durand-Deacon's coat, along with papers referring to the Hendersons and McSwans. They also found a .38 Enfield revolver and eight rounds of ammunition. Pathologist Keith Simpson conducted an investigation into some sludge found at the workshop and discovered three human gallstones and part of a denture – which was later identified by Mrs Durand-Deacon's dentist.

Haigh was arrested and charged with murder. He tried to convince the authorities that he was mad, claiming that he drank the blood of his victims. Haigh was found guilty and sentenced to death. He spent his last days in the condemned cell at Wandsworth Prison and was hanged by executioner Albert Pierrepoint on 10 August 1949. Haigh bequeathed his clothing to Madame Tussauds' Chamber of Horrors, specifically for the wax figure they would make of him. He sent instructions that it must always be kept in perfect condition – the trousers creased, the hair parted and 1in of shirt cuffs showing.

25 JULY   **1899**   Edward Bell, the 'Spalding Poisoner', was executed at HMP Lincoln on this day. Bell (26), a farm labourer, had lived with his wife, Mary (30), and their two children, in a cottage on Weston Marsh. Bell had been having an affair with a young woman named Mary Skeels Hodson at Gedney, and plainly wanted his wife out of the way so he could be with her. In April 1899, Bell's wife had become ill, and died in agony a few days later. It was proved that Bell had bought some chloride of mercury just a few days beforehand. Bell had also bought some strychnine and given it to his wife, saying that the doctor had prescribed it for her. At the inquest, the jury found Edward Bell responsible for the murder of his wife and he was sent for trial at the Lincoln Assizes. Having heard the case, it took only two minutes for the jury to return a 'guilty' verdict against Bell; he was sentenced to death. Newspaper reports commented:

> The execution was carried out in private [by William Billington] but the condemned expressed no contrition for his terrible crime and his conduct during his incarceration was characterised by the same indifference as he displayed at the trial.

26 JULY   **1817**   Elizabeth Warriner was executed at Lincoln on this day. Warriner had been brought before Lincolnshire Lammas Assizes, indicted for the murder of her stepson, John Warriner (11), at Surfleet the previous November. From the time of her marriage to farmer Joseph Warriner, witnesses had commented on how Elizabeth treated the boy with 'great

cruelty', adding that on more than one occasion she had been heard to say, 'I shall be the death of him.'

On the fatal morning, the lad had eaten a breakfast of bread and milk and was taken extremely ill shortly afterwards. The doctor was sent for but, despite every effort, the boy perished. Those who had seen the boy immediately before he died believed that he had been poisoned – and investigations revealed this to be the case. Farmer Warriner kept a supply of arsenic for farm use, and traces of the poison were found in the bottom of the bowl from which John had eaten his breakfast. Elizabeth Warriner was the prime suspect and there was little to be said in her defence when she was brought to court. Found guilty, when the death sentence was passed she jumped up in the greatest agony, wrung her hands and 'exhibited other symptoms of distraction'. Claiming her innocence to the bitter end, Elizabeth Warriner was executed upon the New Drop at the castle. She left three children – one of whom had been born as she awaited her trial within prison walls.

1849 John Ward was executed at Lincoln on this day for the murder of his mother, Martha. A contemporary report stated: **27 JULY**

> No sooner had the wretched convict reached the scaffold ... he became dreadfully convulsed and upon his partial recovery he confessed to the sheriff that he shot his mother intentionally on account of her interference about the servant girl Susan Baggs. When asked if he had made a full confession, whether he was truly sorry and penitent [about] the parricide he replied in emphatic tones, 'Yes.' The bolt was then drawn and Ward appeared to die without a struggle. An estimated 10,000 were present to witness the execution, many of them were women.

Joseph Bowser was also executed on this day, in 1897. Bowser had been a respectable farmer and overseer of the poor in Donington, near Boston. However, his second wife Susan was to suffer badly from one of his horrific drink-fuelled outbursts. He had dragged Susan into the yard with the words, 'I shall shoot her if she aggravates me any more.' He had fired once and missed, then had closed in and fired directly at her head. Found guilty of murder, he was executed by James Billington at HMP Lincoln.

1891 Arthur Spencer (22), a pork butcher from Blythe, lodged with widow Mary Garner in Stanley Place. He was attracted to her but the   **28 JULY**
feeling was far from mutual and so he moved out. When he returned for the last of his possessions, he brought a pistol with him. He had been some time up in the room when he began calling out that he could not find his things. Mary went to investigate and two shots rang out. One shot killed Mary but the second bullet, despite entering Spencer's skull, failed to kill him. Tried and found guilty of murder, Spencer remained indifferent to his fate and was executed by James Berry on this day.

James Berry,
executioner.

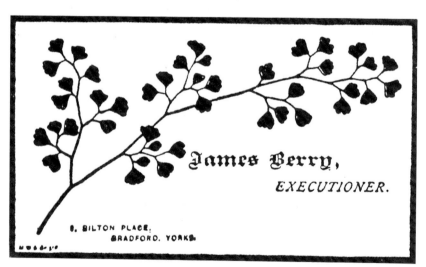

The calling card of
the executioner.

29 JULY 1831   Swing rioters, Richard Cooling and Thomas Motley, were
executed at Lincoln. The so-called Swing Riots were the result of a
widespread uprising of agricultural labourers in the south and east of
England. The rioters were protesting about their poor wages, the tithe
system, poor law guardians and tenant farmers, who were forcing down
their wages and bringing in more and more labour-saving machinery.
Across Lincolnshire, incidents included incendiary fires of corn stacks in

Alford, Easton, South Reston, Swaby, Spalding, Spilsby and Stickford. In response, the gentry armed themselves, and local magistrates maintained constant reports with the Secretary of State.

Cooling and Motley were the unfortunate rioters who were caught and made examples of for setting fire to a beast shed containing a quantity of farm implements and some oat straw, the property of John Cherry at Lusby. The footprints found at the scene had been traced to Cooling, and Motley was soon implicated. When taken before a magistrate, they made a statement that amounted to a confession of their guilt.

1847 On this day, Mary Ann Milner hanged herself in her cell at **30 JULY** Lincoln Castle; it was the eve of her execution. Mary Ann, described as 'a good looking and rather lady-like young woman', had been indicted on

An Account of the Trial, conviction and Condemnation of M. Ann Milner, at Lincoln Assizes July 20th, 1847 for the Murder of Hannah Jickells at Barnetby le-Wold.

Mary Ann Milner, aged 27, was charged with having wilfully murdered Mary Milner at Barnetby-le-Wold in the parts of Lindsey, by administering a quantity of arsenic. After a very long trial of six hours, his Lordship summed up, when the jury consulted for a few minutes and returned a verdict of not guilty.

The prisoner was then arraigned a second indictment charged with the murder of Hannah Jickells on the 25th of June, by administering poison.

Mary the wife of William Winter said she lived under the same roof as the deceased although in a separate house. She saw the deceased on the 23th of June who was in good health at that time; in the evening deceased went to Kettleby, and the prisoner who was her sister-in-law went into her house to her husband, she remarked it because it was a strange occurrence—next morning she saw the deceased who was in good health, at about half-past 8, and saw her again at 10. She afterwards went into her house and found her down upon her knees vomiting violently, and declaring she was poisoned by eating pancakes at the prisoner's. Witness held her head, afterwards she assisted her up stairs where she continued very sick—she was so weak as scarcely to be able to speak, but complained of her throat and mouth, which she said were very hot; she was thirsty and appeared in great agony, as she frequently threw herself up and down the bed—she asked for her husband and he came home at about 1 o'clock—saw the prisoner at about half-past two o'clock and said Hannah Jickells has been eating pancakes along with you and has been poisoned with them. Prisoner turned white but made no answer. She then told her that deceased said so. Eliz Thompson was by at the time this was said. Witness then went to deceased's bedroom followed the prisoner deceased was throwing up very violently, prisoner said to her "do you think I would put anything into the cakes and poison you?" deceased made no answer—she asked deceased if she had taken anything herself, deceased replied she never had any poison in her house. She several times declared she should die as she had been poisoned by eating the pancakes—deceased died at 6 o'clock that evening. She (the witness) ordered her daughter to throw away that which the deceased had thrown up into a wash tub, her daughter did so. the deceased also threw up in some other vessels, and she ordered that to be saved for the surgeons to analyze, and particularly told the prisoner not to throw it away; it was however thrown away and upon asking the prisoner why it was thrown away, she replied it was offensive to the room; the vessels were well cleaned out. Prisoner was in the room when the deceased died, and remarked that she died like her poor mother Milner and deceased's child which had died on the 15th of June. On the day deceased died the prisoner came to her house and said that as she (deceased) had no fire would she have some pancakes with her at her house for breakfast, she (the prisoner) had some, and could easily try another for deceased, deceased said she was very fond of them, she had been thinking of frying herself one but had no eggs, and would therefore go to prisoner's house.—The prisoner at the same time said, "Hannah does not blame me in the least for putting anything into the cakes."

Elizabeth Winter the daughter of Mary Winter, remembered the day deceased's death; saw her in the morning of that day in the garden, she was in good health and spirits at that time it was 9 o'clock; saw the wash-tub and emptied it, there was something like bread or pancake in it with phlegm, she threw it on the ash hill, and afterwards pointed out what she had thrown there, to some men who took it up.

William Booth, a shoemaker in company with G. Watson, searched a dunghill and was shewn by Elizabeth Winter, a quantity of matter, which he delivered to the constable Mackerell.

Constable Mackerell received the matter and gave it to the coroner and afterwards to Messrs. Patteson and Moxon.

Wm. Percival a shop-keeper at Barnetby-le-Wold knew the prisoner; sold her 2 oz. of arsenic when she applied for it, he said it was an awkward sort of thing to sell, but as she was not a person likely to kill herself he did not object. She said she wanted it to kill mice, and that the dog got that which she before had, and he died in the most excruciating agony. He recommended the antimonical wine for the deceased.

Mr. James Burdett Moxon, a surgeon residing at Glandford Brigg, attended the deceased and found her vomiting and purging, she was so weak she seldom spoke, but complained of pain in her stomach. He was suspicious of poison at first seeing her. Prisoner and her mother Sarah Jickels were in the room. He asked the prisoner a question relative to the cause of the deceased's illness, the prisoner said she had had some pancakes with her, and then he examined the matter which the deceased vomited and it looked like partly digested food. He applied several tests all with similar results, which quite satisfied him that arsenic was in the stomach to the amount of 30 grains: 10 or 12 grains was quite sufficient to kill any person, 4 grains had been known to kill a person.

Mr. Milner made a very eloquent appeal or behalf of the prisoner, and the Judge summoned up, dividing the evidence into sections. The Jury must be convinced that the deceased died from the effects of poison, and his lordship then read over, and commented upon, the evidence of the surgeons. The next question was how was it administered and recapitulated the evidence relative to the cake, and then, if the poison was administered in the cake, was it done by the prisoner, and intending to murder the deceased—upon all these points the jury must satisfy themselves and return the verdict accordingly to the evidence.

The jury consulted for some minutes and then returned a verdict of Guilty.

During the whole trial the prisoner remained firm and collected, nor did her demeanor alter when the jury returned their verdict, or when his lordship passed sentence.

In passing sentence his lordship alluded to the dreadful crime of murder, and said he confessed he almost felt to tremble for the security of our lives, and of the continuance of trial by jury, if the gentlemen had came to any other conclusion, than the one they had just expressed, after the careful and minute sitting of the evidence: for how many other murders she might have committed it was not for them to determine, for her crimes she would have to seek intercession for mercy with her Maker. She seduced her unfortunate victim under her roof to partake of her hospitality, and in the face of one of her children administered her poison and sent her to her long account. It was hardly necessary in this case to say that on this side the grave she need not hope for mercy, and advised her to employ the time she had to live, in seeking instruction which would assist her in reconciling her with her God whose laws she had so outrageously violated. His lordship then in a very solemn tone of voice sentenced the prisoner to Death.

R. E. Leary, Printer, 13 Strait, Lincoln.

A broadside recounting the case of Mary Ann Milner.

three separate accounts of wilful murder. She had administered arsenic to her mother-in-law Mary Milner, her sister-in-law Hannah Jickels, and her niece Ellen Jickels. Her father-in-law had also been poisoned by her hand, but had recovered, only to be 'reduced to imbecility from the effects of poison'. Her crimes had been committed in June at Barnetby-le-Wold, near Brigg. The only apparent motive was to obtain payouts from a burial society. Mary Ann was cleared on the first count of murder, but there was conclusive evidence that Hannah Jickels had died from eating a pancake containing arsenic, which had been given to her by Mary Ann. After a deliberation of twenty minutes, the jury returned a verdict of 'guilty'. The third indictment for the murder of her niece was not proceeded with. Mary Ann never evinced the slightest emotion, nor shed a single tear, throughout the trial.

31 JULY 1898   An accident that had befallen Arthur Doades (15) was reported upon. Doades had been in a field scaring birds with a gun when, in the act of reloading the weapon and ramming down the charge, the gun had exploded. The ramrod had entered his forehead and had exited through the top of his head, carrying his cap away for some distance. He was found in an unconscious state and, at first, no hopes were entertained for his recovery; his brain was protruding and paralysis had occurred down one side of his body. The young man was removed to Spalding Johnson Hospital and it was considered remarkable that he was still alive.

AUGUST

A burial at the crossroads.

A Stake Driven Through the Heart

In early August 1796, accounts were published of the inquisition held at Ruskington before coroner George White, on view of the body of George Rowston, an apprentice to blacksmith Thomas Lunn. Rowston had hanged himself with a chain in his master's shop. The verdict of the jury was suicide and, in accordance with the law, Rowston's body was interred by the public highway. Until the 1850s, those who committed suicide could not be buried in consecrated ground. They were taken to a separate, distant area in the north of the churchyard, where the body would be interred face-down, facing west. Many believed that the restless spirits of suicides would 'walk', to harass those they had left behind. Consequently, the bodies would be buried away from the population, at a four-way crossroads, so that the ghost would not know which path to take to return. To ensure that the body and ghost stayed down, the corpse would be chained and 'pinned', with a wooden stake driven through their heart (a practice only prohibited by Act of Parliament in 1823). Crowds would gather around the local sexton as he performed this duty; even children would risk the wrath of their parents by creeping along and looking through the legs of those assembled at the grim rite.

1 AUGUST   **1896**   Coroner Iveson held an inquest at Gainsborough upon the body of Caroline Smith (56), a married woman living apart from her husband. The deceased had been addicted to opium eating for the previous thirty years, and had left the Gainsborough Workhouse Hospital because she could not obtain opium there. She had sent a child with her last three-halfpence to obtain a small quantity of opium, and had been found dead in bed the following morning. Her death was the result of inanition, which is a common consequence of opium use. The jury returned a verdict in accordance to the findings.

2 AUGUST   **1844**   Eliza Joyce (31) was executed at Lincoln Castle. Joyce, the wife of a Boston gardener, had already been before the magistrates in 1843, accused of administering arsenic in a bottle of medicine and killing Edward William Joyce, her son-in-law. In that instance she had been found 'not guilty'. In this new case, Joyce pleaded guilty to poisoning 18-month-old Emma Joyce (the child of her husband by a former marriage) and 6-week-old Ann Joyce (her own child by this marriage). Eliza had confessed to these crimes in Boston Workhouse and, when brought before the court, pleaded, 'I am guilty.' On being sentenced to suffer death, Eliza Joyce 'tranquilly suffered herself to be removed from the bar'.

On the morning of her execution, Eliza was decently attired in a black suit with a black bonnet; she carried a prayer book in her hand. She walked across the green to the north-east tower with tolerable firmness, being only occasionally supported by the two gaolers who were escorting her; the castle bell tolled throughout. Having ascended to the top of the tower, her bonnet was removed, her arms were pinioned, and the cap was placed over her face by executioner William Calcraft. The effect of her appearance on the crowd of over 10,000 spectators was striking; in an instant, the hooting, bellowing and imprecations were hushed, and a profound silence reigned throughout the living mass. The chaplain (to the surprise of all) did not attend Eliza on the platform, but read the usual portion of the burial service at the foot of the steps instead. The signal was given, the drop fell as the clock tolled twelve, and Eliza Joyce was launched to eternity.

William Calcraft, executioner.

1887   An extraordinary incident, which had taken place at Louth during the United Methodist Free Church Conference, was reported. It was stated that about 120 ministers and lay representatives had suddenly suffered the symptoms of poisoning, and fears were raised that some mass poisoner had been at work. Medical professionals were summoned, as were the police; however, no fatalities occurred and the cause of the sickness was traced to a meal of which they had all partaken, and in particular to some green peas, which had undergone the process of fermentation and were believed to have been the real culprits.

3 AUGUST

1872   Reports were published of an inquest held at Grimblethorpe, touching the death of Mr H. Nicholson (59), a well-to-do farmer of 600 acres. He had strolled into his orchard with his shotgun and was found with nearly the entire left side of his head blown off. He left a widow and ten children. The unfortunate farmer had shown signs of 'mental aberration' for some time; in his pocket was a note that stated:

4 AUGUST

> Send to Louth at once, my dear wife. The police will get money from the bank to pay the labourers. God have mercy on you and I dare hardly add on me. Kiss the dear children. There is above £20 in my pocket. I am mad or insane at this moment, my soul does not blanch or swerve.

The jury returned a verdict of 'deceased destroyed himself whilst of unsound mind'.

1859   On this day, the last public execution in Lincoln occurred. On 21 March, Henry Carey and William Pickett had been brought before the Lincoln Assizes charged with the wilful murder of William Stevenson (64) at Sibsey. Stevenson had been for a drink at the Ship public house, about half a mile from his home. Unfortunately, he had been followed in by Edward Sands, William Pickett and Henry Carey. After a short while, a dispute had arisen between Stevenson and Sands, but the situation had appeared to calm down and Stevenson had even treated them all to some beer. At about 10.30 p.m., Carey and Pickett had left the pub and Stevenson had left three of four minutes later. As Stevenson walked home, he had been set upon by Pickett and Carey, who had violently knocked him to the ground with hedge stakes and proceeded to stamp on him. They had then thrown the old man into a ditch. He had managed to crawl out onto the bank, bloody and raw, but his assailants had returned and beaten him about the head until life was extinct, and had then thrown him back into the ditch. Both Pickett and Carey were soon apprehended, and the marks left on Stevenson's body matched their boots.

5 AUGUST

    At their trial, they claimed that they had only meant to rob Stevenson; they got away with the sum of £1 3s 6d. Both men were found guilty and the death sentence was passed upon them.

The execution was carried out by William Calcraft atop the Cobb Tower before a crowd estimated to be not less than 25,000. People had come to Lincoln by rail and all manner of vehicles to see this spectacle, and crushing became dangerous; luckily, Calcraft performed his duties swiftly and there were no injuries among the crowd. Carey and Pickett had black caps placed over their faces; the bolt was drawn and both were launched to eternity. It was recorded: 'Pickett struggled for about two minutes but Carey scarcely moved.' The condemned cell confessions of both men were published in the press and upon broadsides after their execution.

The double execution of Carey and Pickett atop Cobb Tower at Lincoln Castle.

6 AUGUST   **1813**   George Turner Rowell and Azubah Fountain were executed at Lincoln on this day. Robert Fountain, a gardener, lived quietly with his wife Azubah and his family in a cottage in Waltham. He had taken in George Rowell (23), a cooper by trade, as a lodger. Somehow Rowell, a slim-built native of Melton Mowbray with a bad character, and with a face much pitted by smallpox, had endeared himself to the Fountains' eldest daughter and, fatally, to Mrs Azubah Fountain (36). Both parties in this latter, illicit, relationship had conspired to get rid of poor Robert. Rowell had bought a quantity of laudanum from Mr Bennet's Chemist of Great Grimsby and, while he and the Fountains were drinking elderberry wine, Azubah Fountain had slipped 4 ounces of laudanum into her husband's drink. Poor Mr Fountain had soon become very ill and, the following day, Azubah had mixed a further 8 ounces in a cup of ale, which she had given to her daughter Jane to take to her father. Robert Fountain had died later that day and the poorly thought-out stories given by Azubah and Rowell simply did not hold up; the pair were brought before the Assizes. After hearing the case, the jury had hardly retired for two minutes before they returned a guilty verdict and the pair were sentenced to death.

Taken in a cart to the gallows near the city (the site is now occupied by a small roundabout leading onto Burton Road), Rowell and Fountain joined in prayers with the clergyman for a short while then they ascended the fatal steps; Azubah's heartrending sobs were heard by many in the crowd as she did so. The ropes were adjusted, the steps thrown down and off they went to eternity. After hanging for about an hour, their bodies were cut down and removed to a building in the castle yard for dissection.

7 AUGUST

1892 Reports were published of an inquest held at the Red Cow Hotel, Boston, on the body of Miss Ellen Stones (25), the daughter of Robert Stones the butcher of Wide Bargate. Miss Stones had been depressed for some time. On the day of her death, she had helped her father to prepare for church but, soon after he had gone, she had taken a knife from the shop, gone into the upstairs water closet, bolted the door and cut her throat. Her brother had found her – still alive. Although Dr Pilcher was sent for, Ellen died within a few minutes of his arrival. The jury returned a verdict of 'suicide while in a state of temporary insanity'.

8 AUGUST

1829 The case of Mary Ranson (40) was reported. Mary had been brought before the Lincoln Assizes, pleading guilty to concealing the birth of her illegitimate child by throwing it into a water closet. She was afterwards arraigned, on the coroner's inquisition, for the murder of the child. However, as no evidence was offered on the part of the prosecution, the jury returned a verdict of 'not guilty'.

9 AUGUST

1875 Louth tanner, Peter Blanchard, was executed for the murder of Louise Hodgson (22). The couple had been dating for some time but Louise had tired of Peter and wanted to break off the engagement. As Louise was leaving the chapel in Louth with her parents and a young male friend of the family, Mr Campion, Blanchard had joined the group and walked with them back to the Hodgsons' home. A row had escalated and Louise had shown Blanchard the door, whereupon he had suddenly drawn out a butcher's knife and stabbed her in the chest; the knife had penetrated her heart, killing her instantly. Blanchard fled but was soon apprehended by the police. Upon capture, he had asked the officer if the girl was dead and, on receiving confirmation, had replied, 'I am glad.' He later added, 'I did it and I'll die like a man for her.'

Blanchard was tried at Lincoln Assizes, found guilty and sentenced to death. He acknowledged the justness of his sentence and said he wanted to die. He departed with the words, 'Good-bye my dear fellows; I am quite resigned and hope to meet you all in heaven.' William Marwood, the executioner, sent him on his way.

10 AUGUST

1892 An inquest was held in Grimsby, before borough coroner Dr Moody, upon the dead body of an unknown man who had been found lying partly in the water beneath the fish dock jetty. The body was much decomposed and the face was badly disfigured from a blow. There was a photograph in his pocket but this did not lead to identification. It was supposed that the body may have been that of an excursionist who had come to Grimsby from an inland town. The jury returned a verdict of 'found drowned'.

11 AUGUST 1813   A fire in Colsterworth was reported. Loose straw in the yard of Mr Jackson, of the George Inn, had caught fire after someone had incautiously fired a gun in the yard. The fire had immediately spread to a barn and consumed about twenty quarters of beans in a matter of minutes. A stable and two hovels, and even some pigs, had also fallen victim to the flames.

12 AUGUST 1954   Harold Fowler was executed at HMP Lincoln. Fowler (21) was an engineer's labourer living in Flewitt Street, Nottingham. He had been having an affair with Mrs Doreen Mulligan. After falling pregnant, Doreen had moved out from the home she shared with her husband, Kenneth Mulligan (28). When Mulligan had gone to see his wife to collect some items from her new flat, a row had erupted. Mulligan had struck Doreen; Fowler, in response, had stabbed Mulligan with a double-edged dagger. Fowler was found guilty of murder, sentenced to death and sent to the gallows with Albert Pierrepoint as executioner.

13 AUGUST 1810   Isaac Bowers (50) was brought before Lincoln Assizes. He had already been sentenced to seven years' transportation for stealing pigs, but had effected an escape by means of a rope that had been thrown over the prison wall. Sentenced to death 'for being found at large before the expiration of term', Bowers was fortunate to have his sentence commuted to transportation. He was sent to New South Wales for the rest of his life.

14 AUGUST **Cures of Cunning Folk in Fen and Wold: Ague**
Ague, known as malaria in modern medicine, was a common problem in fenland in the past. One treatment for the condition involved the sufferer going alone to the four crossways at night. As the clock struck twelve, they were supposed to turn around three times and drive a ten-penny nail into the ground up to the head, then walk away from the place backwards before the clock finished striking. However, the next person to pass over the nail would become ill in their stead.

Perhaps some preferred the cure offered by wearing live spiders in a bag around the neck, or crushing the spiders and their webs into pill or paste. Others would be prescribed nine worms, to be taken at midnight from a churchyard sod, chopped up small and then eaten. If all else failed, the sufferer would be recommended a mix of rum and laudanum.

1857 The case of Elizabeth Littleover (22) was reported on this day. Elizabeth, a notorious, disorderly character, was brought before the Louth Police Court charged with being an inmate pauper in the Louth Union Workhouse and refusing to work. She was sentenced to be committed to the House of Correction at Spilsby for forty-two days.

1808 Richard Long (19) was brought before the Lincoln Assizes charged with maliciously maiming and killing a mare, and maiming two other mares with a sheep hook; the beasts were the property of his master, Edward Robinson of Silk Willoughby. The motive for Long's barbarous actions was revenge upon his master for disposing of the services of his sister and his mother. Long was sentenced to death but his sentence was commuted to transportation for life.

1891 The case of John Cheseldine was reported on this day. Cheseldine was brought before Horncastle Petty Sessions charged by the police, under the Vagrancy Act, with sleeping in a stable at the Crown Inn in Horncastle. Cheseldine swore that he slept there with the landlord's permission and had done so to assist his poor brother by leaving his own bed to let for others. Instead of being moved by Cheseldine's selfless gesture, the magistrate, Mr F.T. Dymoke, committed Cheseldine to prison for seven days. Mr R.E. Boulton, the defence solicitor, applied in vain to Dymoke to reconsider the sentence; the landlord of the inn was ready to swear that he had given Cheseldine permission to sleep in the barn, and had even supplied him with sacks for covering. The lawyer argued that if Cheseldine had permission to sleep in the barn, then there could be no offence under the Act. Dymoke remained unmoved; he refused to hear the witnesses and Cheseldine was sent to serve his sentence.

1810 On this day, John Atkinson, William Marshall, Henry Sawer and Charles Wakelin were all executed in Lincoln. Atkinson, of Walsoken, had been found guilty of uttering a counterfeit draft under the fictitious name of John Wilson, with intent to defraud Messrs Gee and Clarke, bankers of Boston. Edward Robinson, William Marshall, Henry Sawer and Charles Wakelin all received a sentence of death for housebreaking, but only the last three went to the gallows with John Atkinson. In turn, each man addressed the gathered multitude, hoping that their unhappy situation would serve as a warning to others. Wakelin said: 'Sabbath breaking, bad women and idle company have brought me to this untimely end.' Just before the gallows trap fell, Atkinson turned to the clergyman to shake his hand and say a few words. The trap fell and Marshall, Sawer and Wakelin 'seemed to be dead in two minutes' but Atkinson had not fallen cleanly, and 'to the inconceivable horror of all around', Atkinson cried out, 'O, God! Oh God! I cannot die, I cannot die – lift me up.' Immediately, a soldier of the 69th Regiment went to him, lifted him up a little and then hung on to the body as it dropped again, to 'put the poor wretch out of his misery'.

19 AUGUST   1816   George Morgan (25), a Wyberton labourer, was brought before Lincoln Assizes indicted for highway robbery. Mr G.B. Colley testified that, on the evening of 3 May, he had been about a mile from Boston on the Spalding Road when Morgan had met him and pointed a pistol at his breast, demanding money. Colley had given him two pound notes and some silver. The moon was clouded over and the highwayman's features had been obscured, but he appeared very tall and straight and was made remarkable by his very strong Irish brogue. An hour later, Colley had seen a watchman at Boston and had described the man whom he suspected was a 'known character' called 'Irish George'. John Rose, a constable at Boston, had subsequently apprehended George Morgan in the market place and found a loaded pistol on him.

In court, Colley confirmed that he had recognised the voice and build of Morgan; the pistol was also produced and recognised by Colley – even the way it was held by Morgan, with his shaking hands, was noted. Morgan freely admitted that he had suffered with shakes since his army service during the Napoleonic wars. The jury returned a guilty verdict. The sentence of death was passed but was later commuted to fourteen years' transportation.

20 AUGUST   1824   James Wetherill was executed at Lincoln Castle on this day. On the evening of 22 July, William Berridge, a tradesman of Brigg, had been walking back from visiting a relative in Wrawby. Between the hours of eleven and midnight, when he was a short distance from the Brigg toll bar, he had been shot down by a highway robber, who escaped with the few shillings that Berridge had upon him at the time.

On the morning of 23 July, chimneysweep James Wetherill had aroused suspicion when he was observed digging in his father's garden. When the local constable investigated, he discovered that the item which had been so hastily buried was a large horse pistol, showing marks of having been recently fired. Wetherill was apprehended soon after, in a hay field adjoining the town, and was taken into custody. When interrogated about his movements, Wetherill became very sullen. While in custody, he was incautiously allowed to use a knife and fork to eat his breakfast; he distracted the constable who was with him at the time and plunged the knife into his own throat, partly severing his windpipe. Surgical aid was immediately on hand and Wetherill's life was saved. Brought before the Lincoln Assizes, he was found guilty of murder and sentenced to death. However, concern was expressed by prison surgeons about the stability of Wetherill's neck during the execution, and the protracted sufferings his injury might cause. He was left to heal for twelve days and then went to the gallows.

1886 An inquest was held in Spalding touching the extraordinary suicide of butler Matthew Hardy (50), who was found dead in a pit on the estate of his employer, Mrs Everard. A pole lay across the pit and Hardy had drowned himself by leaning along the pole and putting his head underwater, with his body still above the surface. It transpired that Hardy possessed considerable farming property and had suffered pecuniary losses through depreciation in the value of land. This had played upon his mind and had driven the unfortunate man to drink. A bottle of laudanum was found in his pocket. A verdict of 'temporary insanity' was returned.

21 AUGUST

1893 A tragic accident occurred near Luton Bridge, about a mile and a half from Sutton Bridge. A party of visiting Sheffield fishermen, their wives and children, and two local men, were on an angling expedition on the River Nene when a strong gust of wind caught their sail; suddenly the boat capsized, throwing the occupants into the water. The published casualty list named the following: Joseph Burkinshaw, his wife and two sons; Mr Smith; Mr Thompson; and Miss Hazle – all of them from Sheffield; also lost were Edwin Burton the boatman and his son. The only person to survive was Mrs Smith, one of the Sheffield visitors.

22 AUGUST

1605 On St Bartholomew's Eve, a fire broke out and raged for three days in Bourne. No houses were left standing in Manor Street and the distress of the homeless and ruined people was so great that King James I ordered special sermons to be preached in St Paul's Cathedral and other churches, with an appeal for help to relieve them.

23 AUGUST

The fire in Bourne, as illustrated on an early broadside.

24 AUGUST **1866**   Reports show that cholera broke out in West Butterwick on this day. The first to succumb was Hannah Hanson (43), who died after an illness of twelve hours. The following day, Mrs Eliza Hanson (75) also died, twenty-four hours after becoming sick.

25 AUGUST   John Howard Reports on the Prisons of Lincolnshire:

Lincoln City and County Gaol [visited 1776]. Gaoler: Francis Toyn, salary £20. There is a license for beer. This Gaol near the Gate, has one large room for men debtors, one smaller for women, both up stairs; in each a fire-place; with bedsteads so they may not sleep on the damp earth floor. In one of them is a cage for closer confinement when necessary. These prisoners are sometimes taken into the Keeper's house. No court-yard: no water accessible to prisoners, no straw.

An unfortunate scold on a ducking stool.

26 AUGUST   Table of Fees for Lincoln City and County Gaol, settled by the Justices at General Quarter Sessions at the Guildhall, 1759:

Every Debtor that lies in a bed belonging to the Keeper is to pay one shilling weekly and no more.

Any Debtor that finds a bed and [is] placed in the Common Room is to pay nothing for his lodging.

Every prisoner for Debt is to pay one Fee to the Keeper for his Discharge out of prison though he stands committed in several actions and that Fee no more than six shillings and eight pence.

Every Felon is to pay the Gaoler for his Discharge out of prison six shillings and eight pence and no more.

If not continued in Prison above a week then to pay only three shillings and four pence

Every prisoner that will eat with the Gaoler is to pay for his lodging and diet weekly four shillings and six pence having three meals a day.

Every Prisoner committed from the Bar by the Judge of Assize or Sessions is to pay the Gaoler for his Discharge three shillings and four pence and no more.

1859 The harvest in Brigg was in full swing; the weather was favourable and propitious for gathering in the crops. The work and subsequent festivities, however, were marred by widespread instances of chronic diarrhoea in Brigg and the surrounding neighbourhood, which forced the men and women who were assisting with the harvest to avail themselves in hedgerows, or forget all modesty at the most inopportune moments to empty their bowels.

27 AUGUST

1859 Samuel Varlow, a regular offender, was confined in the Caistor parish stocks for the offence of drunkenness. The following evening, a 'large party of rustics' from the town and neighbourhood rowdily spilled out from the White Horse Inn and set about the local policeman in a reprisal attack, inflicting severe injuries upon him. Fortunately, some neighbours came to the rescue and four ring leaders were marched off to the police station.

28 AUGUST

1859 Reports were made of an inquest, held at Caistor Union House, upon the body of inmate John Dann. Dann had been employed pumping water from an open cesspool into a barrel to use on garden land. His workmate had gone away for just five minutes but, during that time, Dann had seemingly been seized by a fit and had fallen into the reservoir, which contained liquid to a depth of about 4ft. He was dead before any assistance could be rendered to him. The jury returned a verdict of 'accidental death'.

29 AUGUST

Punishments of the Past: Cuck Stools and Ducking Stools

30 AUGUST

There is a good deal of confusion between these two punishments; the two terms have blurred over the years and are often used interchangeably. Both stools were widely used for the punishment of minor offences, especially in relation to strumpets and scolds. The cuck stool is far older and features in the Domesday Book. Its use was to publicly expose the miscreant on the stool, often with a sign or symbol about their neck proclaiming their misdemeanour. There is no evidence to suggest that this original punishment was used for submerging offenders in water. The ducking stool was, however, a punishment to be dreaded. Used on scolds and strumpets, the ducking stool was probably sixteenth century in origin. The stool was fixed to the end of a long pole or rope which was attached to a pulley. When the offender was fixed in the chair, the pole or rope was lifted and dropped, as required, by human or mechanical contrivance. The chair and occupant were consequently ducked in the water.

31 AUGUST   **1899**   An inquest was held in Boston upon the body of Arthur Ryan (12), who had been living with his brother in Norfolk Place. Ryan had been in Boston West when a thunderstorm had burst over the district. Ryan was missed, and, when his brother had gone to look for him, he had found him lying dead at the roadside in Middle Drove. The lightning had struck him on the right side of the head and, passing along his body, had burnt out the left trouser knee and slit open his left boot. Under his body, an open clasp knife was discovered, which the deceased had been using at the moment he had been struck. A verdict of 'accidental death' was returned. Other casualties in this storm included two men injured by lightning in Sutterton; a horse killed by a strike in Dr Shaw's field; and a drover named John Green, who had been carrying a pint of beer in Booth's Passage, Norfolk Street, when the lightning had struck the pitcher, cutting it away and leaving the handle in the man's hand.

SEPTEMBER

Changing horses at the Bull Inn on the turnpike.

He Paid his Toll in Full

In September 1790, James Quanborough was found dead in his bed in Bourne – at the grand age of 102. He had been a collector of road and market tolls in Bourne for over forty years and, for that time, had had no other support except on market days, when he went filching and picked up potatoes, carrots, cabbage or horse beans, which he used to boil together with grains. For fourteen years he had not shaved, and for the last seven years of his life he had not been out of his room. When he died, his room was searched and revealed upwards of £300 in a variety of secret locations.

1 SEPTEMBER   **1960**   John Louis Constantine (22) was executed by Harry Allen at HMP Lincoln. Constantine, a box maker, had a room in Queen's Drive that backed onto a shop run by widow Mrs Lilian Parry (76) on Summers Street. During the course of robbing the shop, Constantine had injured Mrs Parry. He afterwards said, 'In my panic I struck out at her and gave her two or three blows with a crowbar.' At his trial, Constantine had tried to blame an accomplice, who had subsequently come up with an alibi. The jury were satisfied that he had acted alone and returned a guilty verdict; he was sentenced to death.

2 SEPTEMBER   **1889**   Fifteen London dock labourers were brought before Bourne Police Court charged with vagrancy. The men were described as presenting 'an exceedingly pitiable aspect' and related a sad story of the poverty and hardships that they had undergone since the strike in London. They had tramped from the docks and were on their way to Hull, seeking work, when they were arrested. They said that they were willing to work but had been barred from employment and were not eligible for relief from the strike fund because they had been brought to London from Dundee. Despite receiving some relief from the vicar of St George-in-the-East in London, they had been left with no option but to seek work elsewhere. Indeed, when they had been searched, a total of little more than fifteen shillings was found among them. The dockers were all committed to Lincoln Prison for seven days with hard labour.

3 SEPTEMBER   **1895**   District coroner, Dr Clegg, held an inquest in Boston concerning the death of Fred Wydell (17), a farm servant working for Mr Alliss in Midville. Wydell had been employed to carry water to a thrashing machine but had changed jobs with another worker, who used a machine for cutting bands. Wydell had reportedly kicked something into the machine and had subsequently fallen in himself. The machine had a safety guard but it had not been closed by the feeder, who had gone to get his lunch. The lower part of Wydell's leg had been dragged off and his thigh was lacerated. Despite being removed from the machine and transported to Boston Hospital, where Dr James Tuxford found it necessary to amputate the leg at the thigh joint, Wydell died as soon as the operation was completed. The jury returned a verdict of 'death from misadventure'.

4 SEPTEMBER   **1883**   Horncastle executioner William Marwood died on this day. Born in the village of Goulceby in 1818, he was the fifth of ten children born to William and Elizabeth Marwood. William's father was a shoemaker and young William had followed into his trade, working from his own premises – a cobbler's shop near the church at Horncastle. The young Marwood had always shown thoughts and intellect beyond many of those in his class. A staunch Methodist, he saw himself as a servant of the world and, aware of the bungling executions carried out by William

Calcraft, he soon set about developing far more humane methods of execution by hanging.

The method of the 'Long Drop' – whereby the condemned had their neck broken by a calculated length of drop, meaning instantaneous death, rather than suffering slow strangulation – was already known, but Marwood was the first British executioner to use the 'Long Drop' and develop the 'table of drops' as a guide for executioners. Marwood is also credited with introducing the split trapdoor for gallows.

Marwood had taken years over his experiments and calculations, and was finally given the chance to carry out his first execution (at the age of 54) upon William Frederick Horry at Lincoln Castle on 1 April 1872. The prison authorities were impressed, and, when Calcraft relinquished his post in 1874, Marwood became Britain's No. 1 executioner. It would be true to say that William Marwood was the first man to treat the job of executioner as a profession and took great pride in his methods, demeanour and efficiency. In fact, it was soon said that Calcraft hanged them but Marwood *executed* them. A popular little rhyme asked:

Plaque marking Marwood's shop and his work as executioner.

> If Pa killed Ma
> Who'd kill Pa?
> Answer: Marwood

Marwood never did write his memoirs, but his story can be pieced together from a number of features about him, from interviews he gave over the years, and from the many letters he wrote; in one of them, from 1879, he explained his methods. In his own words and spelling:

> Sir, in Replie to your Letter of this Day I will give you a Compleat Staitment for Executing a Prisoner –
> 1-Place Pinnion the Prisoner Round the Boadey and Arms Tight –
> 2 Place Bair The Neck –
> 3 Place Take The Prisoner to the Drop
> 4-Place – Place the Prisoner Beneath the Beam to stand Direct under the Rope from the Top of the Beam
> 5-Place Strap the Prisoners Leggs Tight
> 6 Place Putt on the Cap
> 7-Place Putt on the Rope Round the Neck Thite. Let the Cap be Free from the Rope to hide the Face angine Dow in Frunt
> 8-Place Executioner to go Direct Quick to the Leaver Let Down the Trap Doors Quick No – Greas to be Putt on the Rope.

Despite rumours that Marwood had been poisoned in a reprisal for his execution of the Phoenix Park assassins, Marwood's death certificate states that he died from 'Pneumonia aggravated by disease of liver and kidney'. In his nine years as a hangman, he hanged 177 people, among them train murderer Percy Lefroy Mapleton; poisoner Dr George Lamson; axe murderer Kate Webster; Henry Wainwright, who murdered and

The story of William Marwood, illustrated shortly after his death in the *Illustrated Police News*.

William Marwood's cobbler's shop on Church Lane, Horncastle.

dismembered his mistress; and the infamous cat burglar, murderer and all-round Victorian bogeyman, Charles Peace. Marwood was married twice but had no children and his effects, clothes and memorabilia were all sold off; even his gravestone became the target of souvenir hunters – they chipped away bits of it until there was nothing left.

1839 Peter Collins (20), Michael Nestor, and a number of other **5 SEPTEMBER** Irishmen, were drinking at a pub in Branston. By midnight, they were all the worse for drink, and Collins left with Nestor. The pair went to a bakehouse and, shortly after, a quarrel was heard from within. A woman who lived nearby gave an alarm. Upon running to the door of the bakehouse, she saw Collins striking at something with a hoe. He was then seen to pick up a heavy stick and strike again. The woman screamed and Collins ran out. Nestor was found in a sitting position, bleeding profusely from the head. A surgeon was called; one of the wounds to Nestor's head had penetrated his brain and he died little more than a day later. Collins was chased and apprehended. Upon searching him, the change that Nestor had received after buying a beer was found. At the Assizes, a letter that Lord Oranmore had sent from his estate in Mayo was produced, explaining that Collins had been a man of good character and general peaceable demeanour, and that Nestor, whom he had also known, was one of 'very quarrelsome and violent temper'. Found guilty of aggravated manslaughter, Collins was transported for life.

1847 On this day, magistrates investigated the case of Ellen Tuxworth **6 SEPTEMBER** (21), who had left Louth Union Workhouse with her illegitimate 1-month-old baby, Lucy Anne, bound for her native South Thoresby, but had arrived without the child. Despite her denials, local police investigated and found that Ellen had last been seen with what appeared to be a babe in her arms near Manner's Pond in Haugham. When confronted about this, Ellen claimed that the child had died while she was on the road; she had met a man who said he would dispose of it and he had thrown it into the pond. The pond was searched and the poor baby was found a few feet from the bank, naked except for a napkin tied around it. The clothing that Tuxworth had been wearing for her trip was found in a coalhouse where she had lodged – the clothes were still wet and stained with blood. The nurse of Louth Union attested that Tuxworth had frequently beaten and ill-used the child, thrown it onto the bed and repeatedly said that she would 'make an end of it' when she got out of the workhouse, because then she 'should be at liberty to glean a fine sight of the corn this summer'. Mr Bogg, the surgeon, carried out the post-mortem. The tragic babe had suffered stab wounds corresponding with a pair of scissors, and a portion of her tongue had been cut out. At the inquest, the jury returned a verdict – to the surprise of media and observers – of 'wilful murder against some person or persons unknown'.

7 SEPTEMBER   **1846**   Mr Rogers, the master of a respectable boarding house in Louth, brought his boys to Middlethorpe to give them a holiday. After a day spent playing games, a number of boys decided to bathe in the sea – but five of them got out of their depth and were overtaken by the tide. Mr Rogers managed to save two boys at great risk to himself but, sadly, the other three boys, Mackender (17), Gunness (16) and Wakelin (15), were lost. No blame was placed on poor Mr Rogers, who had been supervising the boys with two assistants.

8 SEPTEMBER   **1896**   An inquest was held in Stickney upon the body of Patience Butler (11), who had died from the effects of gunshot wounds. It transpired that the deceased girl had been attempting to take some apples from a tree belonging to Mr Holmes. Holmes's son, Walter William (11), had taken his father's gun to threaten her. The gun had caught upon a fence and exploded, hitting the girl in the breast and head. She had died within a quarter of an hour. The inquest jury believed that it was an accident and returned a verdict accordingly.

9 SEPTEMBER   **1864**   On this day, a fire broke out in Billingham. It was discovered at about 10 a.m. on the roof of a hovel belonging to William Scott, a wood dealer, at the corner of the main street leading to Lincoln. The wind was blowing a gale from the west and the sparks flew in all directions, soon turning into flames that spread to the buildings in the yard and to the outbuildings of Mr Newton the carrier. A brick-and-thatch cottage was levelled to the ground in minutes. The flames then spread across the road in an easterly direction, destroying two more cottages and some buildings that were storing grain. The flames leapt across to another street, destroying more cottages, one occupied by Robert Wilson, the other by John Stevenson. The substantial house of Thomas Gilbert, a stone building with a thatch roof, was completely burnt out, leaving just the walls. The Primitive Methodist chapel was also burnt out, along with a cottage occupied by William Gadsby, and a number of stacks and outbuildings. Among this devastation, William Sharp lost the produce of 4 acres and a number of pigs were also killed. Thankfully, all of the villagers remained safe, but their loss would be a heavy one as many of them had no insurance. Nearly 100 men, women and children had to find temporary lodgings after losing their homes as a result of the fire.

10 SEPTEMBER   **1877**   A smart young man named James White was brought before the Lincolnshire Quarter Sessions on this day. He had lodged for about three months with Mr and Mrs Isaac Vickers at their home in the fashionable suburb of New Clee, Grimsby. Mr Vickers had returned one evening to discover that the lodger, a few of his valuables, and his wife, were gone! A warrant had then been issued for their arrest and very soon a Cleethorpes police sergeant had placed his hand on White's shoulder.

White had buckled immediately and blamed the woman he had eloped with, making the pitiful excuse, 'She persuaded me to do it.' The jury were unimpressed too; he was found guilty and sentenced to six months' imprisonment with hard labour.

1847 A strange discovery was reported. The head, skin and entrails of an ewe had been found in the field of farmer Mr Tongue in Branston; the carcass was never found. A reward of two guineas was offered for the conviction of those responsible.

1844 Boston was visited by a heavy storm of rain, hail, thunder and lightning, the effects of which were felt for a considerable distance around. At about four o'clock, the 'electric fluid' struck a wheat stack containing about forty quarters, the property of Mr Wilcox in Timberland Dales. In less than half an hour, the Tattershall engine was on the spot and upwards of 300 local people gave their help. The flames were contained but would not easily abate and the stack was entirely destroyed.

1844 Reports were made of an inquest held at Chapel Hill, Boston, upon the body of Thomas Atkin (40). Thomas had been driving a wagon drawn by three horses, with himself riding upon the shafts. In the process of stepping down, his smock frock had caught on some part of the tackle, causing him to fall, and the near wheel had passed over his body. The poor man had languished in excruciating torture for five weeks until death relieved him of his sufferings. The inquest recorded 'accidental death'.

1857 The case of Richard Balderson (12) was reported. Balderson was brought before the Mayor's Court in Louth, charged with wandering about the streets. The lad presented a miserable figure – he did not even have a pair of boots or shoes to his name; his back and shoulders bore the marks of severe beatings; and his left arm lolled by his side, shrivelled and useless from the effects of burns. Balderson stated that he had absconded from his home the previous day, having been beaten by his stepfather, John Bean, at Alford, for refusing to gather manure off the road without shoes. The boy was fed and provided with a pair of shoes. The Bench directed the Chief Constable to inform the police authorities at Alford, calling their attention to the matter.

Cures of Cunning Folk in Fen and Wold: Preventing Nightmares

To cure nightmares and ward off the evil eye, Fen folk hung a flint stone with a natural hole in it over the head of their beds. Another remedy was to hang stockings crossways at the foot of the bed, or place shoes carefully by the bedside – 'coming and going' that is, with the heel of one pointing in the direction of the toe of the other. Then they would be sure to sleep quietly and well.

16 SEPTEMBER **1818** An accident was reported in Bilsby, near Alford. Simon Rutland, a wheelwright from Hogsthorpe, was returning from market at about 9 p.m. with some neighbours. They decided to stop at a pub in Bilsby, but Mr Rutland suddenly rode off at speed. He was followed in a few seconds by those who had been with him, and was found to have fallen from his horse. He was groaning deeply as he lay in the road. A surgeon was fetched from Alford with all due haste but, as *The Times* reported: 'The wretched man had expired before he [the surgeon] arrived, having dreadfully fractured his skull.'

17 SEPTEMBER **1850** News was published regarding some workmen in the employ of Mr Hamworth, a surgeon from Lincoln, who came upon three stone coffins while excavating his garden. The area was believed to have once been part of one of the city's old burial grounds. One of the coffins had a slab cemented over it which, when opened, emitted a very disagreeable odour and was found to contain the perfect skeleton of a female. It appeared that the coffin was too small for her, as the shoulders were tightly jammed into it. The newspapers were informed that Mr Hamworth was giving the remains to the Mechanics' Institute.

18 SEPTEMBER **1894** An inquest was held in Gainsborough on the death of John Brook, the former keeper of the Black Head Hotel. Brook had been landlord for ten years but had got into financial difficulties and had taken up business as a game dealer, with extensive connections as a buyer of pigeons across North Lincolnshire. He had been subject to fits and had lately given way to drink. One night, he had returned home intoxicated and had sat up after his wife and child had gone to bed. It was then that he swallowed a quantity of carbolic acid, which he kept in the house for cleaning scales. His wife, who heard him fall, had called a neighbour, but to no avail. The jury returned the kindest verdict of 'death by misadventure'.

19 SEPTEMBER **1906** The Grantham railway disaster occurred on this day. A Great Northern Railway (GNR) evening sleeping-car and mail train was travelling from London Kings Cross to Edinburgh Waverley, hauled by Ivatt *Atlantic* No. 276, when it derailed near Grantham, causing a final death toll of fourteen, with seventeen injured. The accident occurred in mysterious circumstances; the train had run right through Grantham station, where it was scheduled to stop, and had derailed on a sharp curve at the end of the platform. At the inquest, it was agreed that both the driver and fireman were competent men to work the train, but the evidence was not conclusive regarding whether the brakes had been applied in sufficient time to effect a stop at Grantham.

A number of explanations for the cause of the accident have been suggested over the years – such as the driver going mad, being drunk, falling asleep, being taken ill or having a fight with the fireman. However,

RAILWAY SMASH·GRANTHAM 19·9·06

The scene of devastation after the Grantham railway disaster on 19 September 1906.

the clear evidence given at the inquest by signalman Alfred Day, who was at the south box, a quarter of a mile from Grantham station, was that, although the train appeared 'to be running too fast to stop at the station', he had seen both men standing looking forward through the cab front windows, apparently calmly and in their normal positions. This opinion was echoed by Richard Scoffin (who had been in the employ of the GNR since 1890). He had been in the north cabin at the time, 129 yards from the north end of Grantham station platform. At the inquest, both train driver Frederick William Fleetwood (45), and fireman Ralph Talbot (23), received unreserved reports of good character, competency and reliability from Mr Martin Cole, the District Locomotive Superintendent at Doncaster, who had known both men for a number of years. No definite cause of the accident was ever established; indeed, it has been described by some railway historians as 'the railway equivalent of the *Marie Celeste*'.

20 SEPTEMBER   1850   An experimental trial with bloodhounds belonging to the Lincoln Association for the Prosecution of Felons was reported. A dog was taken to Messrs Setteringtons' farm near Clay Bridge and was given the scent of a person who had killed a sheep. The hound, after taking a circuitous route, traced the man through Stainton Wood, across farmland, highway and the Manchester, Sheffield & Lincolnshire Railway line. It then made to the river, crossed it and picked up the scent again, until reaching George Olivant's farm in Scothorne Grange – a trail of some 3 miles. It was here that the dog found the sheep's head, much to the gratification of the members of the association and those interested in the case.

21 SEPTEMBER   1889   The case of Elizabeth Smith (59) of Brampton was reported. Smith was a habitual smoker and laudanum drinker, who was also prone to fits. Some neighbours had noticed smoke issuing from her house and, upon opening the door, had found her body in bed, burnt to a cinder. Officially it was thought that Mrs Smith had been smoking in bed and had been seized by a fit, which had caused her pipe to fall from her mouth and set her clothes alight. Curiously, little regard was paid to the fact that there had not been major damage to the bedclothes, apart from in the immediate area of the fire.

22 SEPTEMBER   1884   The self-proclaimed 'Baron' Blaquiere, a begging letter impostor, was brought before Gainsborough Police Court on this day. Since a recent appearance at Worksop, he had been held in Lincoln Prison and was liberated upon the receipt of £5 from the Duke of Portland. Since his arrival in Gainsborough, the police had industriously looked him up and found that he had been to several Lincolnshire county magistrates, offering the Duke's letter as a guarantee of his respectability. He had asked for money at the house of local JP, Mr Pearson, and had urged the donor to regard the sum as a loan. He was soon serving fourteen days' hard labour at Lincoln Prison.

23 SEPTEMBER   1864   Reports were made concerning Ann Kitchen's trial. Kitchen was a domestic servant, in the employ of George Stamp, a farmer at Newton By Toft. At the trial, Kitchen pleaded guilty to the charge of stealing a £5 note and a gold ring, the property of her master. She was committed to Kirton House of Correction for two months with hard labour.

1864   Reports were published of the inquest held before Dr Sharpley, in the Board Room of the Louth Union Workhouse, upon the body of Michael Harrison, a young Irishman. The inquest was held in consequence of rumours that Harrison had received violent treatment at the hands of another Irishman, named Corrigan. Thomas Topham, a miller, was chosen as foreman of the jury and, after the jury had viewed the body, the evidence of Mr Bogg the surgeon was taken. Surgeon Bogg proved that the death had not been the result of any violence but rather scarlet fever and inflammation of the lungs. Indeed, the poor fellow had been suffering for some time and had not been able to take care of himself. When admitted to the Union, the surgeon had seen that his case was hopeless. Death 'from natural causes ... and not from any violence' was recorded.

24 SEPTEMBER

Plague

25 SEPTEMBER

The Black Death (bubonic plague) was one of the deadliest pandemics in human history, and is estimated to have killed around half the population of Europe between 1348 and 1350. Characterised by the appearance of buboes in the groin, neck and armpits, that oozed pus and bled, accompanied by headaches, fever, aching joints and vomiting, most victims died within four to seven days of catching the infection. The Black Death broke out in Lincolnshire in September 1348 and spread through the county. Within months, a third of the population was dead and this once prosperous and well-populated part of agricultural England lay devastated.

Cures of Cunning Folk in Fen and Wold: Nosebleeds and Cuts

26 SEPTEMBER

To cure bleeding from the nose, a red cotton or ribbon was tied around the neck of the afflicted, with nine knots down the front. If the patient was male, the ribbon was put on and tied by a female, and vice versa. To cure bleeding from cuts, a thick cobweb or puff-ball was applied to small wounds, such as those acquired while shaving.

Strange Tales and Folklore of Lincolnshire: The Legend of Bayard's Leap

27 SEPTEMBER

A witch named Old Meg lived on Ancaster Heath with her two malformed children or 'cubs'. She was the bane of the local countryside, causing the crops to wither and livestock to die. Abner, an old soldier who had returned from the wars, was at the time working as a wagoner in Ancaster

village. Resolving to rid the countryside of Old Meg, he rode his old warhorse Bayard to her hut and called her out, sword in hand. Upon his call, she replied, 'I'll buckle my shoes an' suckle me cubs, an I'll soon be with yer, me laddie.' When she came out, the soldier slashed at her and cut off one of her breasts. She sprung upon the horse and dug her nails in so viciously that Bayard made three enormous leaps – but neither soldier nor witch fell off. Then the soldier turned and thrust his sword through Old Meg with such force that it went into Bayard, and both witch and horse died on the spot. Across the heath, the marks of Bayard's mighty horseshoes were cut into the earth; the location is now marked with metal horseshoes.

28 SEPTEMBER Punishments of the Past: The Birch

The birch consisted of a bundle of leafless twigs from a birch tree. No specific number of twigs have been recorded for the construction of the birch, but most surviving examples from provincial areas are made up of between fifty and seventy young twigs. The instrument would have been about 3ft long. The cut ends of the twigs were bound together with cotton cord to make a handle, the flexible twigs terminating in the natural ends which would deliver the punishment.

The birch was reserved mostly as a corporal punishment for wayward boys found guilty of petty offences, from the medieval period up to the twentieth century. Adult males found guilty of crimes against the person, such as robbery with violence, could be sentenced to receive a flogging, also known as 'the lash'. In convict parlance, flogging was referred to as 'a bashing'. This punishment was also used on convicts who seriously transgressed prison rules by, for example, assaulting a prison officer. The Governor could not summarily order a prisoner to be flogged; the case would be brought before the Visiting Justices and the transgressor would be punished according to their order.

Administering a birching.

Strange Tales and Folklore of Lincolnshire: Divining a Witch

29 SEPTEMBER

In the past, if somebody had good reason to believe that they were bewitched, then they might have tried pulling hair from their head and placing it on a frying pan, then cutting one of their fingers and letting some blood fall on the hair. The pan would be held over the fire until the blood began to boil and bubble. A witch was then expected to knock at the door three times, wanting to borrow something and hoping to make the sufferer talk. If they uttered a word, they would become more bewitched; if they refused to speak, the witch would be caused such pain that she would beg forgiveness – and then they would be set free.

30 SEPTEMBER

1750 On this day, earthquake tremors were felt in Bourne and the surrounding area. In his *Collections for a Topographical, Historical and Descriptive Account of the Hundred of Aveland* (1809), historian John Moore recorded:

The houses tottered, plates and glasses fell from the shelves, and slates, tiles and some chimneys fell from the houses; but happily, no great mischief was done. In some churches where services were not over, the people ran from their devotions in the utmost consternation. The shock was attended with a rumbling noise.

OCTOBER

Henry VIII left no doubt about his contempt for the Lincolnshire Rising.

The Lincolnshire Rising

The Lincolnshire Rising began at St James' Church, Louth, on 1 October 1536. In the wake of the closure of Louth Abbey, the uprising was against the Dissolution of the Monasteries and the suppression of Catholic religious houses, and was not against the King or the Church. The rising rapidly gained support in Horncastle, Market Rasen, Caistor and other nearby towns. Religious protesters were joined by those demanding an end to taxes in peacetime, the end of the Ten Articles, an end to the Dissolution, a purge of heretics in government and the repeal of the Statute of Uses. With support from local gentry, a force of demonstrators, estimated to number around 40,000, marched in Lincoln and occupied the cathedral, demanding the freedom to continue worshipping as Catholics and gain protection for the treasures of Lincolnshire churches. The uprising effectively ended on 4 October 1536, when King Henry threatened the occupiers to desist or face the forces of the Duke of Suffolk. The protesters dispersed by 14 October, but a number of the ring leaders and others were hunted down and punished. Among them, the vicar of Louth was hanged at Tyburn, as were six monks from Bardney and a lawyer from Willingham – who received the full force of the punishment for treason by being hanged, drawn and quartered for his involvement. The Lincolnshire Rising was not in vain, for it did help to inspire the more widespread Pilgrimage of Grace.

1890   An inquest was held at the Gatehouse Inn, Bracebridge, upon the body of Joseph Clayton (21), a wagoner in the employ of William Arden of Skellingthorpe. Clayton had been to Lincoln and, upon his return, he had been in charge of two horses. Whilst riding on the shaft of the cart, he had been thrown off and the wheels of the cart had passed over his head, fracturing his skull. A verdict of 'accidental death' was returned.

1854   Joseph Ralph made his escape from Lincoln Castle on this day. Ralph, a notorious burglar, had been convicted at the last Lincoln Assizes for breaking into the Grimsby Bank, and had been sentenced to be transported for twenty years.

NOTICE.

ESCAPED

FROM LINCOLN CASTLE,

On the night of the 2nd instant,

JOSEPH RALPH,

Under sentence of Transportation for 20 Years.

He states that he is a native of York, and served an Apprenticeship to a Stonemason named Johnson; he is about thirty years of age, but looks older; he is five feet six and a quarter inches high, has a round full face, fresh colour, small mouth, rather small blue eyes, a small mole under the left eye, and one under the left ear, and a cut on the left cheek: he has light brown hair, inclined to curl, rather bald on the top of the head, short neck and broad shoulders, a cut on the back of the left hand, a blue mark below the left elbow, and is very reserved in his manner. He had on when he escaped, a pair of dark grey prison trowsers tied up the sides with tape, but took with him a Brown Melton Over-coat, a dark coloured Alpaca Jacket, the sleeves of which are nearly new and darker than the body, and a Waistcoat of the same material; a pair of faded Black Cloth Trowsers, and a Black Hat. He was double leg ironed, and handcuffed to his left wrist.

☞ *Information is to be immediately given to the Keeper of Lincoln Castle, or to the nearest Constable.*

Lincoln Castle, Oct. 3rd, 1854.

W. AND B. BROOKE, PRINTERS, LINCOLN.

Escaped! The notorious burglar Joseph Ralph making one last bid for freedom.

There were two keys to the cell where Ralph was held; one was kept by the turnkey and the other by the chaplain. When visiting the prisoners, the chaplain often placed his key on the bench and, observing the key, Ralph had made an accurate drawing of it. A small gas light burned in his cell, which was also furnished with a pewter mug. Ralph had made a mould of the key from chewed bread and had melted the mug into it, forming the key. The door of the cell had a wicket about the centre, which was within reach of the lock outside. This small wicket closed with a spring. The night before his escape, Ralph had intercepted the spring so that he could introduce the key to the keyhole when he was ready.

On the morning of his escape, he opened his door, proceeded to the kitchen and stole some clothing belonging to the cook. He passed some iron gates, drew the bolt, and shot the lock on the principal entrance, thereby reaching the castle yard, which was enclosed by a mound and a high wall. Despite being in irons, he managed to get into a small building and obtain a ladder, by which he got over the castle wall.

The following day, posters were produced seeking information about the escaped prisoner. Despite his best efforts, Ralph was not at large for long and was soon apprehended, after putting up some desperate resistance, by a rural policeman in the suburbs of Nottingham. Ralph was subsequently returned to Lincoln Prison.

3 OCTOBER   1884   Sarah Ann Sharpe, a domestic servant, could not seem to hold down a position. Her mother-in-law, Elizabeth, wanted her to try for another job, but all she got in reply was a tirade of extremely offensive language and even threats to 'do for her'. Sarah was brought before Lincoln City Police Court, charged with using obscene language in Cross Street, and Elizabeth Sharpe was placed in the witness box. A letter was passed to the Bench in which Elizabeth's daughter-in-law had threatened to murder her. It was recorded as 'a most disgusting production, overflowing with obscene language'. Sarah Sharpe was sent to the Quarter Sessions.

4 OCTOBER   1863   Reports were published of a terrible accident at Mr Simmond's oilcake mill in South Street, Boston. Mrs Wright had gone to the mill with her daughter, niece and a number of other young people, to observe the method of transforming linseed into oilcake. The whole party had been standing in a doorway while the foreman of the works explained the operation. Suddenly, one of the presses had broken with a tremendous crash, and a heavy iron bar was hurled at the group. Young Miss Maria Wright had received the full force of the blow upon her head, and her skull was fractured in a frightful manner. Her mother and cousin were also struck by the iron and knocked down, and a little boy standing nearby was injured. Poor Miss Wright had died the following morning; her cousin soon recovered but, at the time the story was published, the situation of Mrs Wright 'was despaired of'.

1864   Reports were published of a large fire on the Lincolnshire 5 OCTOBER
side of the Humber Bank, upon the farmstead of John Stephenson
of Warren House near Burnham, one of the largest farms in North
Lincolnshire. The fire had broken out at 7 p.m. and continued to
illuminate the sky until midnight. Local opinion was that the fire had
been started deliberately by a vengeful incendiary; a newspaper report
added, 'The horrid nature of such diabolical revenge – judging from
some expressions of opinion that were heard in the neighbourhood –
scarcely met that detestation it deserved.'

1887   Reports were published of the inquest held at Lincoln Prison 6 OCTOBER
upon the body of Catling Henson (47), a married man who had
been incarcerated since the last Lincoln Assizes, when he had been
sentenced to fifteen months' hard labour for firing a stack at Tydd St
Mary, Long Sutton. Soon after his admission to the gaol, Henson had
complained of dizziness. This had discontinued and he was put to work
on such labour as he could do. Subsequently, he had suffered a slight
stroke and his mind became unhinged; an order was obtained from the
Home Secretary for his removal to the County Lunatic Asylum but, on
the morning that the order arrived, Henson died. A verdict of 'natural
causes' was returned.

1811   In October 1784, James Sadler (1753-1828) made the first 7 OCTOBER
ascent by any English aeronaut, with a 170ft hot-air balloon which he
had constructed himself.
   On 7 October 1811, during a flight accompanied by a Mr Burcham,
Sadler set a balloon speed record as a gale swept their balloon 112 miles
away in eighty minutes. The *Gentleman's Magazine* reported:

> Mr. Sadler, accompanied by Mr. John Burcham of East Dereham, made his 21st
> ascension from Vauxhall, near Birmingham, amidst an immense concourse of
> spectators. The process of filling the balloon (which was 40 feet high by 50 wide)
> was completed by two o'clock, and 20 minutes after, it rose rapidly, steering North
> East by East. In about three minutes, they were enveloped in a cloud, which they
> soon cleared, when the aeronauts were at a sufficient height to have an extensive
> view of the surrounding country; Lichfield, Coventry, Tamworth, and Atherstone.
> In the neighbourhood of Leicester, the wind shifted due East, and in that direction
> they proceeded towards Market Deeping, in Lincolnshire, when the aeronauts were
> at their greatest elevation (about two miles and a half); from thence they saw the
> towns of Peterborough, Stamford, Wisbech, Crowland, &c. Mr. Sadler, perceiving a
> current of air passing under him to the Northward, deemed it prudent to descend,
> in order to avoid being carried toward the sea. The balloon now quite distended,
> it became necessary to let out some of the gas, which was done at intervals, till it
> descended into the current Mr. Sadler had previously noticed; and the adventurers
> were carried directly Northward. Spalding was now on their right, and Bourne

A contemporary engraving of James Sadler's balloon ascent.

on their left, when they threw out their ballast. The car first struck the earth at Boston, to the Southward of Heckington, with extreme violence, the grappling irons being ineffectually thrown out; and on the second concussion, Mr. Sadler, having hold of the valve-line, was by a sudden jerk, caused by the grapple taking hold for an instant, thrown violently out, and unfortunately received several contusions on the head and body; but, notwithstanding, had sufficient presence of mind to call out to Mr. Burcham not to quit his seat.

The balloon immediately rose, about 100 yards, with great velocity, to the great hazard of the Gentleman who remained in it. At length he succeeded in pressing the bag of rarefied air, sufficiently to occasion the balloon to descend again; and throwing out the grappling-iron, in the parish of Asgarby about a mile and a half from the place where Mr. Sadler was thrown out, it came in contact with a tree, which stopped its progress; and Mr. Burcham was fortunately relieved from his perilous situation, and safely landed on terra firma with only a slight bruise. The aerial voyage was completed at 40 min. past three, being one hour and 20 min.

from the moment of ascension, having in that short space traversed a distance of at least 100 miles. Mr. Sadler lost both his flags; and the balloon was nearly destroyed.

Each aeronaut had given the other up for dead and they were delighted to meet in the flesh at the village of Heckington, shortly after their mishap.

1817   Thomas Hall, an elderly man aged about 70, and his housekeeper, Mary Grant, a woman of about the same age, were discovered murdered on this day at their lonely cottage in Theddlethorpe, about 12 miles from Louth; it was later ascertained that they had been killed the previous night. Newspaper accounts described how they had been 'most inhumanly murdered by some diabolical monster'. Both had suffered multiple stab wounds from a butcher's knife and their mangled bodies were discovered upstairs, their blood dripping through the floorboards onto the furniture downstairs. The killer had entered the cottage by making a hole in the back wall, intent on robbery, but had clearly been disturbed by some of the men returning from their harvest supper and had fled empty-handed. After a few days' investigation, John Raithby appeared to be a likely suspect and, after being committed to prison upon the coroner's inquest on 16 October, he voluntarily and fully confessed his guilt. He confirmed that he had acted alone and had gone to the house intent on robbery only, but the elderly couple had put up such resistance that he had ended up killing them both. Raithby was sent to Lincoln Castle Prison and was racked with guilt. Within the prison walls, he remained in almost constant prayer, 'his agony of mind, accompanied with visions of horror, continued day and night till nature sunk under the conflict', when he died in late December 1817. The inquest returned the verdict that he 'died from excessive grief'.   **8 OCTOBER**

1892   David Naylor (13) was employed in the surgery of Dr Sadler in Spring Gardens. The boy had a good character but had been visited by the police in connection with a charge. He was last seen on the bank of the River Trent, where he told some boys who were fishing that he intended to throw himself in the river. Nothing more was heard from him and, at the time of reporting, it was feared that he had carried out his threat.   **9 OCTOBER**

1884   Reports were published of a case brought before the Kesteven Sessions in Lincoln. George Albans, a wagoner in the service of farmer Charles Topham at Doddington, was charged with appropriating 40 stone of wheat to feed his master's horses. Mr G.E. Jarvis, of Doddington Hall, stated that a dead horse from Topham's farm had been sent to his kennels and he had noticed that the stomach of the animal was quite full of wheat – and was so hard that a man could stand upon it. He had at   **10 OCTOBER**

once sent for a constable and informed Mr Topham. The horse that had died was worth £40. Other horses were taken ill but they appeared to be recovering. Albans asserted that, in his opinion, the animals had looked poor and he had fed them the wheat to put them in better condition. He was sent to prison for two months as an example to any other who might have similar ideas.

11 OCTOBER   **1897**   Reports were published concerning the findings of the adjourned inquest at Gainsborough into the death of Mrs Burton. Dr Muller, the county analyst, deposed that a mixture that was supposed to consist of citrate of iron and quinine had contained strychnine instead. The mixture had been obtained from a Gainsborough chemist as a remedy for toothache, and the unfortunate woman had taken just enough to cause death. The jury found that death was due to the strychnine having been sent by mistake by a London firm.

12 OCTOBER   **1889**   Reports were published of the inquest held upon the body of Thomas Richard Hides, a farmer from Asperton. On the day of Hides' death, William Dodds, a wagoner in the employ of the farmer, heard screams from the crew yard and, running over, had found his master on the ground with a bull trampling him and goring him with his horns. On trying to enter the yard, the bull had rushed at Dodds, who managed to escape and call for assistance. The young man who answered the call was Robert Ford (17), who kept the bull back with one hand while helping Dodds to remove his master with the other.

Dr Storey deposed that Hides' fatal injuries included fractured ribs and skull, and the left side of his face had been laid open by the beast's horn. The jury returned a verdict in accordance with the evidence. Young Ford was then called forward and was given singular praise by the coroner, who stated that Ford was 'a credit to his parish and the country' and he 'wished Her Majesty's regiments could find many such recruits'.

13 OCTOBER   **Punishments of the Past: Oakum Picking**
Oakum picking was a common occupation set for prisoners during the nineteenth century. The process could be carried out in solitary confinement cells or with other prisoners (in silence) in workrooms or oakum sheds. It involved the prisoner being given a weighed amount of old ships' rope cut into lengths, often black with tar and deeply engrained with salt. After separating the rope into its corkscrewed coils, the coils would be unrolled by sliding them back and forth on the knee, with the palm of the hand, until the meshes were loosened. The strands were then separated and used for caulking the seams in the sides and decks of wooden ships. Men, women and children prisoners all picked oakum; it was very hard on the fingers – rope cuts were common, as were blisters, which proved very painful until the skin on the hands hardened to the

work. Prisoners were expected to produce between 3 and 4lbs every two hours; shifts of oakum picking could last up to twelve hours. Most prisoners would be paid a little money for their oakum pickings – literally money for old rope!

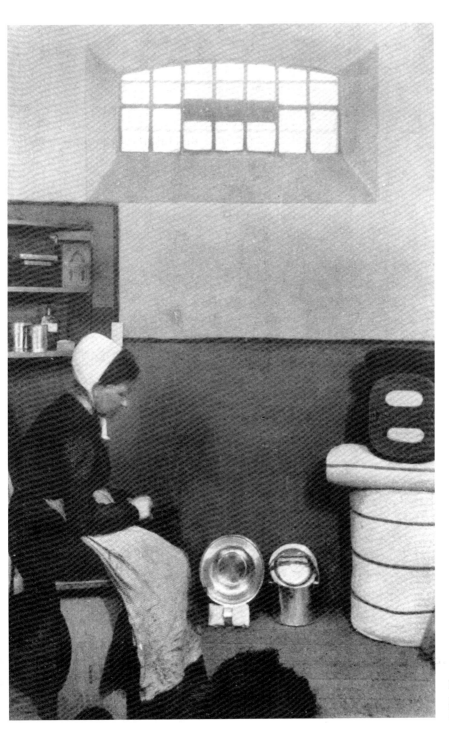

Female prisoner picking oakum in her cell, *c.* 1890.

14 OCTOBER   **1886**   Reports were published of an accident that had befallen Lincoln corn merchant, John Emerson. Emerson had been in the process of storing wood in an outhouse which adjoined his residence at The Limes, on West Parade, when one of the pieces he was throwing inside had hit a beam, rebounded, and struck him hard on the face. His left eye was injured so badly that it had to be removed from the socket.

15 OCTOBER   **Strange Tales and Folklore of Lincolnshire: The Toad Stone**

Ploughmen, horse tamers, bull handlers, horse doctors and snake catchers all had a witchbone to 'charm' the creatures that were key to their occupations. In certain parts of Lincolnshire, such a charm was even believed to give the possessor power over the black arts. Up to the early twentieth century, a 'sacred' faith was placed in the witchbone (also known as the Witch Stone, Toad Stone or Toad Bone). Ethel H. Rudkin recorded an account of the practice from Willoughton in *Lincolnshire Folklore* (1936):

> You take a black toad, an' put it in an ant 'ill, an leave it there while bones is all cleaned. Then take the bones and go down to a good stream of runnin' water at midnight and throw the bones i' the steam. All the bones but one will go downstream, an' that one as wont go down stream is the breast-bone. Now, you must get 'old of this 'ere bone afore the Devil gets it … keep it allus by you – in your pocket or wear it – then you can witch; as well as that, you'll be safe from bein' witched yourself.

The toad – a creature shrouded in mystery and power in Fenland folklore.

Man and bull in harmony – thanks to the Toad Stone.

1818 Coningsby shoemaker, James Baker, died on this day. On the day after his burial, his disconsolate widow went to be married to an Irishman named John Foy. The number of persons assembled at the church to witness the ceremony became so disorderly that the couple could not be married. The clergyman ordered two Peace Officers to attend the following day and the ceremony was then performed. When the newly married couple were returning from church, some of the rioting multitude endeavoured to get a halter around the bride's waist, and they pulled the poor woman about in such a manner that they actually broke one of her arms – to the utter disgrace of themselves and the spectators.

16 OCTOBER

1898 The Wrawby Junction (Barnetby) railway disaster occurred on this day. Five goods trucks, laden with long poles, left the rails; one of the trucks toppled over, fouling the down line at Wrawby Junction on the Great Central Railway, just as the 4.45 p.m. express from Cleethorpes to Manchester was passing. The express dashed over the wagon and was totally wrecked, with the exception of the rear carriage and the brake. Two carriages were swept off their trolleys, leaving nothing but cushions splashed with blood. Six people were killed on the spot and, of the nine who were injured, two did not survive. At the inquest, it was concluded that there was 'no evidence whatever showing gross or culpable negligence' and, at the request of the jury, Kidney (the signalman), Hulse (the driver) and Osborne (the fireman) were commended for their prompt actions in attempting to avert the accident.

17 OCTOBER

1889 A curious story was reported from the South Holland Sessions. Prudence Godley Porter, a single woman from Spalding, was charged with stealing £2 12s 6d in money, a silver watch and chain, and other articles

18 OCTOBER

from Clement Corten, the man for whom she worked as a housekeeper. Miss Porter had left the house suddenly and gone to London, where she had entered the Rescue Home of the Salvation Army. The articles were missed and, when she was apprehended, some of them were still about her person. It seemed an open-and-shut case – but Mr Corten said that he did not wish to give evidence against the prisoner. Indeed, he had made arrangements to marry her and the banns had recently been published. The chairman thought this was the 'proper course'; he advised the jury to return 'no bill' and the couple left the courtroom together, shortly to be married.

19 OCTOBER   1864   Martha Pratt appeared before the magistrates in answer to a summons for an assault upon Charlotte Wittaker. Both women lived in Albert Street, Grimsby. From the evidence of witnesses, it appeared that each had reproached the other for bad conduct, whereupon a mutual struggle had commenced, during which their hands had become so entangled in each other's hair that it was a difficult matter for them to separate. The case was dismissed and the costs divided.

20 OCTOBER   **Cures of Cunning Folk in Fen and Wold: Goitre, Wens or other Fleshy Excrescences**
It was thought that various complaints could be cured by passing the hand of a dead body over the affected part on three successive days. Just one touch from the hand of a freshly hanged man would supposedly procure the desired effect, and the hands of a suicide or executed

Touching the hand of a freshly executed man to cure goitre or wens.

murderer were also deemed to be particularly efficacious. In the days of public executions, a hangman could occasionally be bribed to allow a sufferer's wen to be stroked by the hand of an executed felon while he still swung on the rope. This type of action was deeply resented by the crowd, who would boo and jeer at the proceedings. Ganglions that rose upon the hands or feet could allegedly be 'killed' by striking them with a Bible.

1881 The conclusion of the Broughton poaching case was reported. **21 OCTOBER** Labourer John Green (38) had been caught poaching. Whilst being escorted to Brigg in a police cart by Police Superintendent Thomas Danby, Green had asked to get out to relieve himself – but he had immediately run away into Manby Woods. Danby had run after him but, when he caught up with Green, the labourer had thrown Danby down, and kicked and mauled him. A labourer named Bowers had come to Danby's assistance and helped him return Green to the cart. Green was eventually delivered to Brigg. He was found guilty of the assault and sentenced to twelve months' imprisonment with hard labour at HMP Lincoln.

1802 A public apology was published in the *Lincoln, Rutland & Stamford* **22 OCTOBER** *Mercury*:

> I, Sarah Robinson, Wife of John Robinson, baker, Spalding, Lincolnshire, did on October the 1st, 1802, insult Mrs Bridges of Peterborough, Wife of Mr Bridges, Dancing Master, without the least provocation: I hereby declare that the assertions frequently made against the Character of Mrs Bridges representing her being connected with my Husband, are wholly false; and I do hereby publicly ask Pardon, and hope she will not proceed in the Spiritual Court or any other Court against me: those false and injurious Reports having been propagated in the Heat of Passion, for which I am very sorry.

1871 An inquest was held in Gainsborough touching the death of **23 OCTOBER** pork butcher William Johnson, who kept a small greengrocer's on Bridge Street. A person calling upon the business had been surprised to find the door fastened. He had lifted the front window and was horrified to see Johnson lying on his back, with his throat so badly cut that his head only hung on by some sinews at the back of his neck. It was thought that Johnson had had 'domestic troubles which preyed upon his mind'. The deed had been done with a formidable butcher's knife that was found close to the body. The jury returned a verdict of 'temporary insanity'.

Punishments of the Past: Peine Forte et Dure, otherwise known as Pressing for Pleas **24 OCTOBER** English courts were in a quandary if suspects refused to plead; if a prisoner pleaded guilty then the law stepped in, confiscated their estates and meted out punishment – frequently the death penalty. If they pleaded innocence then a trial would ensue, and, if found guilty at the trial, the prisoner would be punished and all possessions were forfeited to the Crown.

Defendants, however, might decide to remain mute. It was not until 1827 that silence by a defendant was construed as a 'not guilty' plea; before that time, their goods could not be touched and, although the accused could be incarcerated, families of the accused enjoyed a degree of protection. This was a powerful incentive for many not to plead. Pressing became the law's equally persuasive method of forcing a plea. The victim would be placed spreadeagled on the floor of a cell; minimal sustenance was given, and, over the course of three days, weights were piled up on their chest, leaving the prisoner with the agonising choice of plead or die.

Pressing for a plea.

25 OCTOBER 1891 An inquest was held in Spalding upon the body of Sergeant Warner, a member of the Spalding Volunteers who had been fatally shot while marking. It was proved that the regulations had been strictly observed and the marker had been shot because he had left the safety area without exhibiting his danger flag. The jury returned a verdict that

Sergeant Warner had been accidentally shot, and wished to add a rider that Sergeant Clifton, who was shooting at the time, was exonerated from any blame. The deceased Sergeant Warner had been married only a few days before the sad event occurred.

1816 The morning light revealed the damage caused by an alarming fire at Belvoir Castle, home of the Duke of Rutland. It had commenced in a room temporarily occupied by the carpenter, where some timber had been placed close to a fire to dry. The wood had caught fire and the flames had spread rapidly, gutting the centre of the building and destroying many precious items of furniture and irreplaceable paintings. The oldest parts of the castle were reduced to rubble, but much of the more modern building remained standing. The alarm was raised in good time and all children and servants were evacuated safely. The Duke and Duchess were away visiting the Duchess Dowager in Cheveley at the time. The Grantham troop of yeomanry cavalry arrived to protect the valuable articles that had been rescued from the fire but were scattered about the grounds in all directions.

26 OCTOBER

1896 Reports were published concerning the case of labourer Albert Brewitt, who had been brought before Lincoln City Police Court. The previous Saturday night, Brewitt had got drunk and threatened to knock landlord Edward Stamp's brains out. Brewitt was about to strike him when Mrs Harriet Stamp had stepped between them and suffered the blow herself, cutting her lip. Brewitt had carried on his attack upon the landlord and knocked him down, hitting and kicking him while he was on the floor. The police were called and, when the constables arrived, Brewitt had struck out and kicked them too, biting PC Culpin on the wrist when he managed to lay a hand upon him. PC Lilburn was also badly bruised during the attack, and PC Clay was tripped up – his leg was sprained so badly that he had to take to his bed for a few days. Brewitt was found guilty of assault and was sentenced to four months' imprisonment with hard labour.

27 OCTOBER

Tales of Lincolnshire Smuggling: The Skeg Owlers

28 OCTOBER

Skegness was a notorious place for smuggling, and one of the leading 'owlers' there was Thomas Hewson. A tailor by profession, after a few forays into the world of smuggling, he found he had developed a taste for it and left his family in his native Anderby to become a 'free-trader'. He gained a fearsome reputation for cunning and deception. One incident, among other dark deeds, which almost brought him to justice, was when a young man of Sloothby mysteriously disappeared. Investigations revealed that Hewson had lured the lad away from his employer and, when he was caught and searched, he was found to have a watch belonging to the youth about his person. However, the body of the man was never found and no further witnesses came forward, thus *corpus delicti* was declared and Hewson walked free again.

29 OCTOBER   **1860**   Reports were published concerning Mark Hughes, alias Burke, a felon who had escaped from the Louth House of Correction. Hughes was under a sentence of four years' penal servitude for stripping a man named McAndrew of his clothing in Louth. When tried for this offence, several previous convictions had been proved against him. Indeed, he appeared to have been a most desperate character.

On the night he escaped, Hughes' supper had been taken to his cell between six and seven o'clock in the evening, and, about twenty minutes later, he had been missed by a warder named Boldock. An outcry had at once been raised and it was discovered that Hughes had got over the palisades that divide the yard from the garden. Running to the end of the garden nearest the priory, he had thrown over a rope (with some hard substance at the end to fix to the copings) and had then climbed over the wall. He had had a companion part of the way, but the other felon had been unfortunate at the outset, having been spiked in his attempt to climb the palisade. Because he had some companions in Horncastle, it was thought that he would make his way there, and Police Constables Wilkinson and Plaskitt were at once sent in that direction. They returned the following day without obtaining the slightest clue concerning his whereabouts but, as he was a well-known character, it was thought unlikely that he would be at large for long. A reward was offered for his apprehension.

30 OCTOBER   **1889**   Thomas Clarke was brought before Lincoln Magistrates charged with attempting to steal a coat worth £1 6*d*, the property of pawnbroker Hugh Shaw. Clarke pleaded, 'I hope you will be merciful to me, I only came out of prison this morning after doing fourteen days.' Previous convictions were recorded, so the Bench had no option but to send him back to gaol, this time for one calendar month, with hard labour.

31 OCTOBER   **All Hallows' Eve**
A night for ghoulies, ghosties and long-legged beasties! Probably the most famous and most prolific of all East Anglian ghosts is the huge spectral dog, often known as Black Shuck, which is referred to simply as the 'Black Dog' in Lincolnshire.

This big black beast has been seen at many locations in the county, over many centuries. One of the earliest recorded sightings was by Henry of Poitou, Abbot of Peterborough, who saw huntsmen and a huge pack of spectral Black Dogs near Stamford in 1127. In Lincolnshire, Black Dog manifestations appear to be more frequently associated with ponds, pits, bridges and water than in other parts of the Eastern Counties. A typical Black Dog appearance occurred by Blyborough pond in the

The Black Dog of
Lincolnshire.

nineteenth century; a lady visitor attempted to fend the creature off with
her umbrella which, to her horror, simply passed through the beast. On
another occasion, local character Sammy Prettywell attempted to shoot
at the dog – but his gun exploded and he narrowly escaped serious injury.
The Black Dog has also been seen upon and around the bridges at Brigg,
between Manton and Scotter, and at Willingham. Other accounts tell of
Black Dogs near the churches at Algarkirk, Kirton-in-Lindsey, Gunthorpe,
Wrangle and Willoughton. In this last location, in 1933, a man was
leapt upon and pushed up against a gatepost by what he believed to be an
invisible dog. Those who have witnessed the manifestation often describe
the dog as being between the size of a large calf and a horse, with eyes 'as
big as tea sorsers' that stand out in the darkness as if illuminated by the
coals of hell. Those who have sensed, but not seen, its presence, claim to
have felt it pass by or press up against them; the bristles of its coat have
been described as 'more of a hog than a dog'. Unlike many of the other
spectral dogs of East Anglia, the Black Dog in Lincolnshire, although a
formidable creature, is not seen as malevolent. A number of accounts
even describe how the Black Dog has made its presence known in order
to ward off footpads, or those intent on committing dark deeds against
the lonely traveller.

NOVEMBER

Dr John Dee (1527-1608).

The Remarkable Dr Dee

Dr John Dee was rector of Long Leadenham in Lincolnshire from 1566 until the end of his life. A man of vision, mathematics and science, he rose to prominence and was accepted into the influential circles around Edward VI. With the accession of Queen Mary, Dee lost popularity and was briefly imprisoned in 1555, accused of using enchantments against the Queen. He was reinstated after the accession of Elizabeth I in 1558 and became her philosopher, and an advisor to the Crown on calendar reform and astrological events. He wrote *The Perfect Arte of Navigation*, and was one of the founders of scientific cartography in England. Dee was an alchemist, hermeticist, cabalist and was adept in esoteric and occult lore. In 1582, Dee took Edward Kelley into his household. Kelley began to act as Dee's medium and joined him in occult research, seeking contact with divine spirits. Kelley is famously said to have performed an act of necromancy, whereby he dug up the corpse of a newly buried woman, then, using diabolical incantations, reanimated her body and forced it to speak.

1455 Rosamund Guy was walking with Neville Randall, the man to whom she was betrothed, in Irby Dale Woods. Their walk together soon turned into a lovers' tiff which escalated into a violent quarrel – during which Randall saw red and murdered his fiancée, burying her body nearby. Randall fled, but reportedly covered his tracks by sending word that he and Rosamund had gone to Kingston. Years later, Randall returned to Irby to settle some property he had been left, and Rosamund's parents challenged him about their daughter's whereabouts. Randall claimed that they had argued upon reaching Yorkshire and she had stormed off homeward; he said he had not seen her since. Although Randall failed to convince them, Rosamund's parents were unable to prove anything against him. They cursed him and said that if he had killed their daughter, her ghost would appear every year on the anniversary of her murder. The spirit of Rosamund still cannot rest, and is occasionally seen on the open land between Irby and the River Humber. She is known to locals as the 'Irby Boggle'. A curious footnote to this story dates from the nineteenth century, when some workmen were widening a gateway into the wood and, while digging, uncovered a human skeleton – later confirmed to be that of a young woman.

1907 Richard Deering (25) was brought before Lincoln Assizes on this day, charged with the murder of Emily Lockwood at Edenham on 24 July. Deering was a married man who had left his wife and children in Birmingham in July 1906, claiming he was going to seek employment. He had lodged at the house of Mr Jones in Long Eaton, where he had made the acquaintance of Jones's adopted daughter, Emily Lockwood. She had soon become infatuated with Deering and suddenly left with him to set up home as husband and wife in Melton Mowbray. There, Emily had purchased some oxalic acid and the two had set off, walking by the river to Bourne. Here they had agreed to die together; both took the poison and went into the river. Passers-by went to their rescue but Emily, who had consumed more poison than Deering, was in a bad way. With her last breath, she said, 'I did it myself, it wasn't Dick; don't take him to prison.' A few days later, Deering had recovered and was taken into custody. At his trial, the judge instructed the jury that, according to law, if two persons agreed together to commit suicide and one of them died in consequence and one survived, then the survivor was guilty of murder. The jury returned a verdict of 'guilty' with a strong recommendation for mercy. The death sentence was passed upon Deering but his sentence was later commuted to imprisonment.

1877 'Spring Heel'd Jack Appears in Lincolnshire!' *The Illustrated Police* *News* published the following account on this day:

> The neighbourhood of Newport near Lincoln has been disturbed each evening
> by a man dressed in a sheep skin or something of the kind, with a long white tail

coat. The man who is playing this mischief has springs to his boots and can leap a height of 15 or 20ft. The other night he jumped from a college and got into a window on the roof and so frightened the ladies that one had not yet recovered the shock. Some other people were so much frightened by this object that a very large mob of men armed with sticks and stones assembled and attempted to catch him, but to no avail. The nuisance became so great that two men got guns out, chased him and shot at him as he jumped up the Newport arch but so tough is the hide the shot did not penetrate it and running over the house tops on the other side he escaped but soon appeared in another part of the town. He was again chased and as he was running on the wall of the new barracks he was shot at by a publican, but the shot did not appear to take effect.

The Roman gateway known as Newport Arch, Lincoln, *c.* 1900.

The *Illustrated Police News* depicts Spring Heel'd Jack's appearance at Newport Arch.

1877 On this day, reports were published of a fire in the extensive rick yard of Edward Dawson at Glentworth Cliff. Messengers were despatched for assistance to subdue the flames. In due time, the Lincoln City Fire Brigade (under the command of Chief Constable Mansell) arrived but, due to the limited supply of water and the ricks being nearly burnt through, it was decided to reserve the supply and concentrate upon preventing the fire from spreading to the farm buildings; in this effort they were most successful. In all nine buildings large ricks were destroyed, causing damage estimated between £2,000 and £2,500. Two wagons and a farm cart also fell victim to the flames. The fire was thought to have been the work of an incendiary.

4 NOVEMBER

1877 Reports were published of an inquest held at the Brown Cow Inn, Louth, touching the death of a young girl named Susan Goodrick Storr. Her father stated that 'although she could talk in a certain fashion and walk about, she was no means sharp in her intellect and could not discern one day from another. She required much looking after.' Mr Storr had been in the garden when he had seen smoke issuing from his house. He and his wife had only been outside momentarily and had immediately rushed in to discover that the poor girl was on fire. Mr Storr had extinguished the flames and called for medical help, but the poor child had succumbed to her injuries the following day. The verdict returned was 'accidental death' and the coroner added that he hoped the press would encourage the use of fireguards.

5 NOVEMBER

1876 There was a 'Guy Fawkes' riot in Bourne on this day. On the night of the celebrations (the traditional night of 5 November fell on a Sunday this year so the revelry was held off until Monday), the police station was attacked by roughs, and the constables were compelled to retire within. The town, then in the possession of the mob, suffered fires, and fireworks flew about in all directions. Shortly after midnight, sixteen constables charged the mob in the market place. Several civilians and members of the police were severely injured. The windows of the police station were smashed and order was not restored until daylight the following morning. The cases arising from the riot were brought before Brigg Petty Sessions. PC George Rowson, stationed at Worlaby, was fined 5s plus £1 15s 6d costs for severely assaulting a youth who, it was claimed, was not taking part in the riot and was still suffering from the effects of the blow. Nineteen youths were charged with rioting and assaulting the police. Those accused of breaking windows were discharged; all other defendants were fined 15s 6d each, including costs.

6 NOVEMBER

1850 Eliza Smalley (17) worked as a house servant for Farmer Page at Stow and had always been well treated – until this day, when the farmer's wife, Mrs Frances Page, came at the girl 'like a bulldog'. She had also

7 NOVEMBER

recently accused the girl of killing a fowl, something Eliza swore she had not done. The arguments ended but the matter festered with young Eliza and, knowing that the farmer used a solution of arsenic for dressing wheat and that the pot was outside the kitchen door, she took half a pint out and boiled it in the coffee for her master and mistress's breakfast. Her intention was just to make Mrs Page ill. Both of the Pages, however, were taken with a sudden sickness; Mr Page recovered but Frances was stricken and died in agony about twenty minutes later. At her trial at Lincoln Assizes the following March, Eliza Smalley was fortunate. The jury believed that she had not intended to kill and found her guilty of manslaughter; she was sentenced to transportation for fifteen years. The learned judge implored her to reflect 'both day and night with penitence upon the fatal consequences of the rash and wicked act' of which she had been found guilty.

8 NOVEMBER **1834**   *The Times* recounted a number of recent incendiary fires in Lincolnshire, including a fire in the crew yard of Messrs Jackson and Rudkin's farm near Colsterworth, which had destroyed a barn and a number of ricks. Two Grantham engines, and one from Colsterworth, had attended – but unfortunately there was no water source nearby. The corn destroyed was the produce of 40 acres. Another fire was discovered at a ruinous cottage in Thoresthorpe, on the farm of William Gilbert. His ricks were a short distance away but the wind, blowing gently from the south, had carried the sparks away from the stacks. A correspondent from Folkingham wrote on 5 November:

> I am sorry to say we have had several fires within the last week. Last night we could discover two between Grantham and Stamford. We had a dreadful incendiary fire at a house in Deeping Fen. Mr Bee, an honest and inoffensive man, had everything destroyed – ricks, barns, live and dead stock, dwelling house etc, to the value of £1,000. The evil spirit is reviving with a vengeance as the labourers have got it into their heads that there is to be no more hanging for burning.

9 NOVEMBER **1862**   An inquest was held in Gainsborough concerning the death of John Arnold of the shipbuilding firm Smith & Arnold. Mr Arnold was well liked and had received much acclaim for his work on the construction of the ships *Columbine* and *Harlequin*, the fastest on the river. He was an excellent swimmer, had saved the lives of a number of people and had been presented with a silver cup for his rescues. So the manner of his death was met with some surprise. He had returned home one lunchtime, had spoken to his wife and had then lain down on the sofa, where she left him. A short while later, she had heard a noise upstairs and went to investigate. She had discovered John in a pool of blood on the floor. Thinking that he had ruptured a blood vessel, she had sent for Mr Lowe the surgeon. With his arrival, the sad truth was revealed; John had cut

FREE PARDON.

ARSON IN NORTH LINCOLNSHIRE.

WHEREAS Fires have lately occurred on the premises of Mr. JOHN STEPHENSON of Thornton Curtis, Messrs. HUNTSMAN of Barton-upon-Humber, Mr. EDMUND DAVY of Worlaby, and Mr. JOSEPH JOHNSON of Appleby, all in the County of Lincoln, which are believed to have been caused by Incendiaries.

NOTICE IS HEREBY GIVEN, THAT

HER MAJESTY'S PARDON

Will be granted to any Accomplice (not being the person who actually set fire to the property) who shall give such information and evidence as shall lead to the discovery and conviction of the Incendiary or Incendiaries in any of the cases above mentioned.

BY ORDER,

JOHN HETT,

Clerk to the Justices acting at Brigg.

Brigg, 7th February, 1845.

WILLIAM CRESSEY, PRINTER, BOOKSELLER AND STATIONER BRIGG.

A free pardon offered to find the arsonists responsible for the stack-burning outrages during the mid-nineteenth century.

his own throat with a razor and was dead. The jury returned a verdict of 'temporary insanity'.

Tales of Lincolnshire Smuggling: The Infamous Jim Waite

10 NOVEMBER

James Waite of Ingoldmells was one of the most infamous of all the Lincolnshire smugglers. He had been caught in the act on numerous occasions; his contraband had been seized and three boats had been confiscated and sawn in half – but such incidents only seemed to enhance his folk-hero status. Waite's notoriety can be judged from the fact that Skegness coastguards carried a portrait of the man in their watchboxes, entitled 'James Waite, the notorious smuggler'.

11 NOVEMBER **Strange Tales and Folklore of Lincolnshire: The Boggart of Jenny Hurn**
Not far away from Owston Ferry is a sharp turn in the River Trent called
Jean Yonde (known locally as Jenny Hurn). This is allegedly home to a
strange boggart of pygmy size, hairy and man-like but with the face of
a seal. It is said to cross the river in a boat similar to a pie dish, with two
spoon-like oars. Once in the field, it browses and then feeds. Superstitious
locals in the past did not like the area, and old keelmen would tell of
'feeling bumps' against the side of their vessel when anchored in the
bight, awaiting the turn of the tide. No keelman would lie there at night
if he could avoid it.

12 NOVEMBER **1892** Emma Foster was brought before Lincoln City Police Court,
charged with committing a serious assault upon an elderly invalid
woman named Harriet Holland in Gaunt Street. Foster said that she
had struck out at the old woman with a brush in anger and without
thought, and said that she was sorry. Dr William Harper Wigham stated
that he had been called to the house and had found Harriet Holland
suffering from two wounds in the forehead – one of which was serious
– and reported that she was now out of danger as far as the wounds
were concerned. Mr Mansell, the Chief Constable, asked the magistrates
to withdraw the case for an indictable offence and substitute one for
assault, which would render it unnecessary for the infirm Mrs Holland
to appear in court. This request was granted. Found guilty, two previous
convictions were found against Foster and she was sentenced to two
months' imprisonment with hard labour.

13 NOVEMBER **The Stamford Bull Run**
In a tradition said to date back to the twelfth century, this day was once
the Stamford Bull Run, when, upon the strike of eleven, a bull was
turned loose into a barricaded street. The bull would then have hats
thrown at it, and be deliberately irritated by various other means, until it
was 'fired-up' and ready to run. The barricades would then be removed
and the 'Bullards' – men, boys and dogs – rushed helter-skelter through
the streets, chasing the bull through the town. One of the aims of the
'sport' was to topple the unfortunate beast from the Town Bridge into
the river. The bull then swam ashore to the meadows, where the run was
continued. The miry, marshy state of the fields at that time of the year,
combined with the falls and other disasters consequent thereon, added
greatly to the amusement of the mob. The pursuit was carried on until
all were tired; the animal was then killed, and its flesh sold at a low rate
to the people, who finished the day's amusement with a supper of bull-
beef. This custom was finally stamped out, though not without great
resistance, in 1839.

Illustration from a Stamford Bull Run broadside.

1892 An inquest was held in Spalding upon the body of James Smith (86). Smith was formerly a farmer in the Weston Hills district, but had latterly lived alone in Spalding. The evidence showed that the deceased had been accused of stealing a chain which he had picked up; it was said that this had had a great effect upon his mind and he had threatened to drown himself. A neighbour had noticed that the house remained shut up later than normal and, being suspicious, an entry was made through a window. Mr Smith was found hanging in a back room. A verdict of 'suicide whilst of unsound mind' was returned.

14 NOVEMBER

1842 A hue and cry was issued after information was received at Bow Street that...

15 NOVEMBER

> ... some evil disposed person or persons maliciously set fire to a stack or stacks on the premises of Mr Thomas Gilbert, The Bull Inn, North Kilworth, Lincolnshire, whereby parts of a stack of barley and a stack of wheat straw were destroyed.

A reward of £25 was offered for the discovery of the incendiaries, and Her Majesty's most gracious pardon was offered to any accomplice who would give the necessary information. On that same evening, two wheat stacks, the property of Mr Joseph Hunter of Baumber, near Horncastle, were likewise set on fire by an incendiary and totally destroyed. A reward of fifty guineas was offered for the discovery of the arsonist.

1866 Reports were published regarding two wheat stacks which had been discovered on fire, and were soon totally consumed, on the farm of James Bingham Swallow at Caistor. The Caistor fire engine had been in attendance, but no water was near to supply the pumps. A third stack had been moved by men of the farm and was saved from the fire. William Hotson, the 10-year-old son of one of Mr Bingham Swallow's labourers, was the only person seen near the place when the fire had broken out

16 NOVEMBER

and, as he had had some Lucifer matches in his possession a few minutes before, he was arrested and taken to the lock-up at Grimsby.

17 NOVEMBER **1887** The Governor of Lincoln Prison received a communication from the Home Office on this day, stating that the sentence of death passed upon Mary Ann Wharrie at the Lincoln Assizes for the murder of her illegitimate child at Sutterton Dowdyke, near Boston, had been respited and commuted to penal servitude for life. Wharrie had delivered a healthy male child at Spilsby Workhouse; a few days afterwards, she had left with the baby. The body of a child was dragged out of a hole in a field soon after. When Wharrie was traced and arrested, she said she had unintentionally given the baby an overdose of laudanum but denied using violence. Medical examination, however, attributed death to injuries about the head. At the Assizes, the jury had returned a verdict of 'wilful murder' and Wharrie was sentenced to death.

18 NOVEMBER **1854** Frederick Spicer escaped from Lincoln City Gaol. His cell was discovered unoccupied on this day, at 6 a.m., during the Head Warder's inspection. The Governor was summoned at once and, with the Superintendent of Police, the escape was investigated. It was soon revealed that Spicer had obtained some sharp, pointed instrument – probably one of the knives used by prisoners – and with this had made a hole (large enough to receive a mop nail about half a foot in length) in the jamb of the door and had then filled the hole with putty. At night, when the cells were locked, he had removed the putty and foiled the lock. Spicer had then ascended to the upper floor, where he had forced a massive lock and procured bed rope from the hospital beds. He had broken into the closet where prisoners' clothes were sometimes deposited and got himself a set of civilian clothes, which he exchanged for his prison uniform. Having accomplished this, he had descended to the lowest floor where a door opened into the yard; a pair of steps here, which had been used for the purpose of cleaning the windows, enabled him to reach a bridge leading to a wall whence he descended into another yard. He had then forced the lock on the gate with an iron fire-rake and reached the east wall, where a tarred rope used by boatmen was put over the wall by an accomplice and fastened by Spicer to some steps. With a long pole, which he had taken from the prison, he had knocked the loose bricks off the wall and, having hoisted himself over the wall and into the Governor's garden, he had made off.

Spicer was finally recaptured in January 1855 in London, after a tip-off in a letter sent by the son of Mr F. Wilkinson of Lincoln, who had recognised Spicer. Spicer had changed his name to Collins and was waiting to be engaged as an under-steward aboard a ship about to sail for Australia. Inspector Ashton was despatched post-haste and, having successfully apprehended the fugitive, returned him to the walls of the prison.

1892   The death of 'Cranky Jimmy' was announced on this day. James Anderton was a born and bred Lincolnshire agricultural labourer who had earned the title of 'Cranky Jimmy' after devoting ten years of his life to the construction of an exact model of Lincoln Cathedral made out of corks, using more than a million in the process. Anderton had engaged in his task after his labours of the day, and walked nearly 3 miles daily to the cathedral in order to perfect the details of the edifice, picking up corks on the road or wherever he might find them. Gradually his fame had widened, and cooks from all parts of the district had sent him their old corks. His work was painstakingly detailed and, after the model of Lincoln Cathedral was completed, he was induced to undertake other works, including a remarkable model of Scott's monument in Edinburgh. 'Cranky Jimmy' became known as 'The Patient Man' and his works were displayed at the Great Exhibition of 1862.

1907   William Duddles was executed at HMP Lincoln on this day. Duddles (47) had lodged with William and Catherine Gear at their home in Lutton Marsh. The relationship between the trio was odd, to say the least, and Duddles had been known to argue with Catherine and even call her a whore; why the Gears had never thrown him out remains a mystery. On the night of 7 October 1907, another row had erupted. William Gear had intervened and hit Duddles; although the latter had tried to fight back, Mr Gear got the better of him. The following day, all seemed 'normal' and Duddles had gone to work. However, when he returned that afternoon, he began a drinking session with a neighbour and another lodger. When all the drink was gone, Duddles left to get more from the Ship Inn, and, on his return, the other two men popped out, leaving him alone with Mrs Gear. When they came back, they found that Duddles had disappeared and Mrs Gear lay dying on the floor in a pool of blood, with a bloodstained coal hammer nearby. Duddles was found leaning on a fence at the Ship Inn; he was extremely drunk, had a black eye and still had some blood on his hands. Found guilty of murder, Duddles was executed by brothers Henry and Thomas Pierrepoint, working respectively as executioner and assistant.

Cures of Cunning Folk in Fen and Wold: Shakes, Fits and Toothache To cure a case of 'the shakes' in the past, one might have cut off a lock of the sufferer's hair and wrapped it around the bough of the 'shivver-tree' (a black poplar in marshland), whilst saying:

> When Christ our Lord was on the cross,
> Then thou didst sadly shiver and toss;
> My aches and pains thou now must take:
> Instead of me, I bid thee shake.

To cure fits was far more straightforward; a strand from a rope with which a man had hanged himself was procured, then always worn around the neck.

Children complaining of toothache might have been given 'their own physic', by rubbing their gums with their own urine while still warm. This is recorded as having a rapid effect.

22 NOVEMBER   **Strange Tales and Folklore of Lincolnshire: The Green Lady of Thorpe Hall**
The 'Green Lady' is said to be the ghost of Donna Leonora Oviedo. Donna met John Bolle, the owner of the Hall, when he was serving with Sir Walter Raleigh at the Siege of Cadiz in 1596. His lordship remained a gentleman towards the beautiful Spanish lady but she fell in love with him and insisted that he took a portrait of her, wearing a green dress, back with him. There are two versions of her sad end: in one, it is said that she killed herself as she watched Bolle's ship leave; in the other, it is claimed that she followed him back to England and Thorpe Hall but, finding her love still unrequited, she killed herself in the gardens. A custom was observed for many years afterwards, that a place would be laid for her every night at the hall for dinner. Despite this remembrance of Donna Leonora, her broken heart was never salved and her ghost is said to haunt the gardens still.

23 NOVEMBER   **1870**   The case of Aaron Mitchell (10) was brought before Welton Petty Sessions. Young Mitchell, whose parents lived in Cottingham, was charged by PC Witty with sleeping in an outhouse in the village. Mr Mitchell, the father of the boy, was in court and stated that he had suffered 'a good deal of trouble' with his son, and admitted striking him at various times. After a short consultation, the Bench ordered the lad to be sent on board the Southampton Training Ship at Hull for five years.

24 NOVEMBER   **1884**   An inquest was held in Gainsborough on the body of Emily Maud Winn (2), the illegitimate daughter of Rebecca Fothergill, who had died from starvation at the Union Workhouse. It appeared from the evidence that Mrs Fothergill's husband was in prison and, since his incarceration, there had been little food in the house so an order had been obtained for admission to the workhouse. Dr O'Connor had found the child in a terribly emaciated condition, with bones protruding through the skin. The child was found to weigh just 11lb instead of the average 2st 6lb of a 2-year-old child at the time. The evidence of the nurse and matron at the workhouse infirmary was that the mother had been systematically unkind to the child and neglected to feed it. When asked if she had been trying to get rid of her child, it was claimed that Fothergill had treated the accusation lightly and laughed. In balance, it was stated that Fothergill was proud – she had tried to survive with no assistance and had said that she would 'rather jump in the Trent' than enter the workhouse. After hearing all of the evidence, the jury returned a verdict that the 'deceased died from want of proper nourishment and maternal care and that such nourishment and care were not withheld with malicious intent'.

1870 John Tyson was brought before the Grimsby Borough Police Court, where he was charged by Sergeant Waldrom with being in the market place with intent to commit a felony. Tyson had been found with a hole through his coat and, when standing in a crowd, was clearly trying to pick pockets. When taken into custody, Tyson had asked in mitigation: 'What is a poor fellow to do when he has no money?' Tyson was found guilty and sent to prison for fourteen days.   25 NOVEMBER

1883 Reports were published of the inquest held at Louth upon the body of midwife Isabella Brown (67). She was nearly blind and her body had been found in a ditch, where she fallen in and sadly drowned. A verdict of 'accidentally drowned' was returned by the jury.   26 NOVEMBER

1888 On this day, there was a great stack fire at Mr Sutton's farm, Spridlington. A light had been spotted near the stack at 1 a.m. and, an hour and a half later, the stack was ablaze. A messenger was sent to Lincoln to summon the fire brigade but it was 5.40 a.m. before they arrived and, by that time, two stacks of straw had been consumed and the fire had spread to two stacks of wheat (the produce of 12 acres) and a seed stack (the produce of 30 acres). The granary had also caught fire but the farm workers had managed to save the corn in it, which consisted of two days' thrashing. The fire brigade could not do anything for the stacks that were already ablaze, but they did manage to save the farm buildings and a stack of barley that stood just outside the stack yard. The origin of the fire was unknown but it was feared that it had been the work of an incendiary.   27 NOVEMBER

Strange Tales and Folklore of Lincolnshire: The Lost Wager   28 NOVEMBER
In 1844, eccentric but well-liked Crowland farmer and churchwarden Henry Girdlestone (56) bet that he could walk 1,000 miles in 1,000 hours. He set off from the Abbey Hotel and returned having completed his journey of 1,025 miles in 1,176 hours – thus sadly losing the bet. His ghostly, tired and dragging footsteps are said to be occasionally heard upon the stairs of the hotel to this day. Henry was not downhearted for too long, however, and, on his 60th birthday, he walked the 60 miles from Crowland, round Thorney Abbey and Eye, and back. Henry completed the walk on a fine moonlit night; many folk had walked alongside him on the way and the Crowland Band turned out to meet him, playing him home to the tune of 'The Good Old English Gentleman'.

29 NOVEMBER   **1892**   Fish hawker Alexander Morgan was charged with the murder of Tom Morley, a Hull grocer, by administering strychnine on 16 August. According to the evidence presented, Morgan had borne a grudge against Morley and had got an acquaintance, George Bennett, to buy the poison for the purpose (or so Morgan claimed) of 'killing dogs'. Morley, Morgan and a woman named Booth, had all gone for a drink at the Newcastle Arms where, after a short while, Morley had been taken ill at 7.25 p.m. He was dead by 8 p.m. As he was dying, Morley had shouted, 'Morgan has given me white powder!' Morgan openly admitted that he had given Morley some medicine and he 'did not think he would want another dose'.

Once in custody, Morgan could only think of his ultimate fate, and said to PC Holliday, 'Hallo, old man; shall you come and see me topped?' adding, 'They do hang them at Lincoln, don't they?' PC Holliday had replied grimly, 'I have known them to do so.'

At the trial, Morgan's defence counsel argued that Morgan had given Morley strychnine 'as a tonic or pick-me-up – something that would sharpen appetite. However blundering or reckless the prisoner, there was no intention to take life.' The judge agreed with the counsel for the defence and, after the jury had retired for just fifteen minutes, they returned a verdict of 'manslaughter'. Morgan was sentenced to twelve years' penal servitude; he wept while the sentence was being passed.

30 NOVEMBER   ### Tales of Lincolnshire Smuggling: The Rights of Man?
Thomas Paine joined the Excise Service in 1762 and, after serving at Grantham, was sent to Alford in 1764, where he was to take up his first responsible position as the Excise Officer for the area. He established his

office at the Windmill Inn in the market place. Paine soon discovered that Alford was a centre for smuggling and, although it was his job to curb these activities, he did so by discouragement rather than punishment. His methods and beliefs did not make him popular with his colleagues – one of them reported him for passing goods on their documentation, rather than inspecting them personally, and he was dismissed. Paine was later reinstated and served as a Customs Officer

Thomas Paine, Excise Officer at Alford and later one of the founders of modern America.

in Lewes, Sussex. In 1774, he made passage to America. Paine became famous for his radical pamphlet 'Common Sense' (1776), advocating colonial America's independence from Great Britain, and later books such as *The Rights of Man* and *The Age of Reason*. Paine became friends with Benjamin Franklin and George Washington, served as Secretary to the Department for Foreign Affairs, and, later, as Clerk to the Assembly of Pennsylvania. He is credited with coining the name 'United States of America'.

DECEMBER

Fillingham Castle, *c.* 1905.

Fillingham Castle
It is said that a ghostly man riding a large white horse has been seen around the grounds of Fillingham Castle. Another ghost, of a previous resident who had been jilted in love and cut his throat on the front doorstep, now haunts the steps and the long corridors of the castle after dark.

Strange Tales and Folklore of Lincolnshire: The Land Lighthouse

Francis Dashwood, 15th Baron le Despencer – rake, politician, one-time Chancellor of the Exchequer, and Lincolnshire landowner – died in December 1781. His only lasting legacy in Lincolnshire was a result of his concern for the safety of travellers on the country roads – a 90ft-tall 'land lighthouse' which he had built high above his estate, between Sleaford and Lincoln. The intention was to shine a powerful light from a large octagonal lantern on top of the tower across the countryside, to deter highwaymen and other rogues who preyed in the darkness. The lantern was regularly lit until 1788 and was used for the last time in 1808, by which time improvements in the local road network had effectively made it obsolete. In 1808, the lantern was destroyed in a storm and was replaced with a 15ft-tall coade stone statue of King George III by the Earl of Buckinghamshire, to celebrate fifty years of the King's reign. The man responsible for carrying out this work was one John Willson, who was killed by a fall from the top of the pillar on 9 September 1810 and is buried in nearby Harmston churchyard. The statue was eventually removed from the old tower; the main portion of it

Francis Dashwood's original 90ft-tall 'land lighthouse', 1800.

The grave of John Willson at Harmston. His memorial stone bears a carving of Dunston Pillar, complete with the statue that proved to be his nemesis.

was made into a bust that now stands in Lincoln Castle. Today the tower stands hollow and gaunt, a shadow of the magnificent land lighthouse it once was.

2 DECEMBER 1847 A melancholy suicide was reported in Cottam. Mr Hall and his family had been sitting down to dinner when their maid, Eliza Bonnington, was missed. A search was made and she was found hanging dead from a rope in the corn chamber. Unrequited love was supposed to have been the cause.

3 DECEMBER 1846 An inquest was held upon the body of Millicent Dixon, a servant of Mr Harland of Branston Fen, on this day. The evidence presented

The tragic end of Eliza Bonnington at Cottam.

at the hearing was described in the press as 'most unsatisfactory'. For some reason that was not forthcoming, Miss Dixon had entered the dairy and, while she was there, the son of her master, Alfred Harland (13), had discharged a gun. The shot had gone through a door that was three fourths of an inch thick and had hit Millicent, tearing away the right side of her neck, baring her jaw to the bone and lacerating her face throughout. Others had instantly come running, and found the walls spattered with blood and Millicent quite dead. Alfred claimed that the gun 'just went off'. The coroner pressed the young man to explain how this had happened. The boy swore that he had not pulled the trigger. The *Lincoln Standard* commented: 'The youth has committed perjury there can be no doubt.' The jury returned a verdict of 'accidental death'. The paper concluded: 'This seems to be a strange perversion of coroner's inquest law, calling for judicial investigation.'

1823   On this day, John Smith (25) purchased 1lb of white arsenic for 9*d* from Mr Robinson, the Alford chemist and druggist. Smith told the chemist that he was going to use it for washing sheep, but he mixed it with some flour and gave it to his fiancée Sarah Arrowsmith (24) who, ignorant of the adulteration, made some cakes with it and presented them to her friends for afternoon tea. In less than a quarter of an hour,

4 DECEMBER

Sarah, her sister-in-law Eliza Smith, her friend and neighbour Mrs Dobbs, and three children – two of them her younger sisters, and one of them Smith's illegitimate child with Sarah – all suffered burning in their throats and excruciating pains in their stomachs. Several medical men were sent for and, immediately on arrival, the surgeons, Mr Tyson West and Mr Pell, set about administering antidotes and emetics. They rapidly had to admit that Sarah Arrowsmith was in a hopeless condition and sent for magistrates to take her deposition from her death bed. Sarah told them who had given her the flour and soon two constables were sent to the cottage where Smith lived in Little Steeping; they arrested him. Sarah died in agony the following day – and with her died Smith's unborn child. Smith was taken to Lincoln Castle where he continued to display 'an entire want of common feeling and appeared quite unconcerned at his dreadful situation'. Two farmers with whom Smith had lived and worked spoke highly of him, describing him as a mild-tempered, sober and industrious man, and a good farm servant. The jury found John Smith guilty and he was hanged before an angry crowd at Lincoln Castle on 15 March 1824. It was commented: 'There was an extraordinary apathy about him to the moment of his exit when he admitted the justice of his sentence.' Smith's body was then passed to the surgeons for dissection.

5 DECEMBER　**1876**　Mr Reasby, the Governor of Lincoln City Prison, returned to his house after a walk, sat down on a couch in his room and died. He left a wife and six children.

6 DECEMBER　**1860**　On this day, Edward Roberts was brought before Lincoln Assizes, charged with setting fire to a stack of coleseeds, the property of Jabez Bailey, in North Kyme. Roberts pleaded guilty. Surgeon Mr George Ritchie deposed that he had known the prisoner for several years and Roberts had complained to him on a number of occasions about pains in the head. Of late, Mr Ritchie was of the opinion that Roberts was not of sound mind and had advised his friends to send him to a lunatic asylum. The judge, Mr Baron Bramwell, accepted the guilty plea and pointed out, 'You knew you were doing wrong and disobeyed the law.' He sentenced Roberts to penal servitude for life, with hard labour, concluding that, in his view, 'Arson is with respect to property almost the same as poison is in respect to life.'

7 DECEMBER　**1888**　Reports were published of a fire that had broken out on the premises of Thomas Page at The Royal Stores, Waterside Road, Barton-upon-Humber. The alarm had been raised by James Downey of the Royal Vaults. Police Sergeant Cobb was soon on the scene, followed by the Barton fire engine. The tide was low in the Haven but the feeding and service pipes had soon been attached and the engine had played on the burning debris – to no avail except to preserve the adjoining buildings.

The loss was estimated to be between £800 and £1,000; the building was partly insured, but not the stock.

1847 Reports were published of the recent proceedings at Louth Police Court. Among the cases were Sarah Sanderson and Elizabeth Ranyard, both of Walkergate, who were charged with being common prostitutes and behaving in a riotous and indecent manner in the streets. Found guilty, they were fined 10s plus costs, or one month in prison if in default. Both went to prison.

8 DECEMBER

1862 James Martin, Charles Cree, Henry Hobson, William Rowbottom, Henry Marriott, Thomas Storr and John Waller were all brought before Lincoln Assizes charged with wounding PC George Greetham with intent to murder him. The men had been out poaching at Scotton; the gamekeepers and local constable had been tipped off and lay in wait. They had encountered the accused men at about 1 a.m. in Mr Oxley's field and the poachers had hurled stones at them. The gamekeepers had fled but PC Greetham had drawn his staff and bravely rushed at them. An unequal fight had erupted; the policeman was knocked down and beaten until he was insensible. He was then pushed through a hedge into a ditch. Gamekeeper Hudson had returned and he too was beaten to unconsciousness. PC Greetham had managed to pull himself out of the ditch and eventually reached home. He was attended by two doctors and remained seriously ill for some five weeks, but managed to identify some of his attackers. Although they were undefended by legal counsel, the evidence against the men at their trial was weak; Martin, Cree, Hobson and Rowbottom were all found guilty of unlawful wounding. Marriott, Storr and Waller were acquitted.

9 DECEMBER

1883 A youth named Charles Wilson was charged at Spalding with assaulting Elizabeth Ann Stubley (14) in Pinchbeck. Miss Stubley stated that she had been walking along the highway with her little sister when Wilson had come across the road, put his arms around her neck and kissed her. She knew the defendant by sight but had never spoken to him or given him any encouragement. Wilson admitted the charge but said he did not think he was doing any harm. A fine of one guinea was imposed.

10 DECEMBER

1951 Herbert Leonard Mills (19) was executed at HMP Lincoln on this day. The beaten and strangled body of Mrs Mabel Tattershaw had been found in a derelict orchard known as 'The Jungle' in Sherwood Vale. Mills had contacted the *News of the World*, arranged a meeting with a reporter, and confessed to the murder. In his statement, Mills said:

11 DECEMBER

> I had always considered the possibility of the perfect crime-murder. I am very much interested in crime and here was my opportunity. I have been most successful. No motives. No clues ... I am quite proud of my achievement.

Mills tried to retract his statement at his trial, but was found guilty and kept his appointment with the executioner.

12 DECEMBER   **1952**   Eric Norcliffe was executed at HMP Lincoln on this day. Neighbours had been concerned to hear a cry of 'Oh, Eric, what are you doing!' at the home of Eric and Kathleen Norcliffe in Warsop. When the police had arrived, they found that Mrs Norcliffe had been stabbed to death. Eric Norcliffe confessed that they had had a savage row when Kathleen had found out he had robbed their gas meter. At his trial, Norcliffe said little; his only significant comment was, 'As far as I can see, the only thing this court has been concerned with is where and when I did it. No one seems bothered why I did it.'

13 DECEMBER   **1922**   The last double execution in Lincolnshire occurred on this day. Frank Fowler and George Robinson met for the first and last time on the gallows at HMP Lincoln. Fowler (35), a farm manager, had been drinking alone and brooding at the White Horse in Market Deeping on 23 September. Fowler was a family friend of newly-wed Ivy Dora Prentice (18), the daughter of the landlady. Fowler had stepped out from the pub, collected his double-barrel shotgun, gone to the side parlour being used by Ivy and her mother, and shot Ivy dead. Ivy's mother had lunged at Fowler and pushed his gun aside, causing the second shot to be fired through the window. Customers had then come running and overpowered Fowler, holding him down until the police arrived. His motive was unclear – he appeared to have a grudge against George Prentice, Ivy's husband; perhaps he was jealous that she had chosen to marry George rather than himself – all Fowler said was, 'There, I have had my bloody revenge.' It was an open-and-shut case and Fowler went to the gallows. He was joined by George Robinson, who had become infatuated with a girl named Frances Pacey. When she had refused to 'walk out' with him, he had lashed out and she was found with her throat slashed in Dorrington. Immediately afterwards, Robinson had cut his own throat and thrown himself in a pond. The cold water had brought him to his senses; he had climbed out of the water, patched his wound and gone home to bed. Questions were raised over Robinson's sanity at his trial and subsequent appeal, but he kept his appointment with the executioner.

14 DECEMBER   **1838**   Concern was expressed in the press over the safety of the roads in Lincolnshire, which seemed to be occupied by 'swarms of highwaymen', making it extremely dangerous for any persons to be on the road after nightfall. Cases cited included that of John Back, a spirit rectifier and wine merchant of London, who was held up on the road near Sleaford. Two men had held his horse's head, two more had sprung upon his gig and violently pulled him back on his seat, whilst others had rifled his pockets and relieved him of £200. Then there was William Ashby, a farmer of Whaplode Fen

End, who had been accosted when returning on horseback from Spalding Fair. He had scarcely left the lamp post near the church when two men had sprung from a gate and seized the bridle of his horse. Ashby was a powerful man and had struck the man to his right with his stick; he was ready to deal similar to the other man when the bridle had broken in the scuffle. Two more men had joined the assault, pulled Ashby from his horse and robbed him of a purse containing four and a half sovereigns, and another purse containing about 15s in silver. Ashby's assailants had then run off into the darkness. It was thought that the same gang (of both women and men) had robbed Mr T. Burnham, a farmer of Spalding Marsh. He had been accosted on the road by two females and had walked with them for a short distance. He had later found himself minus his pocket book containing three £5 notes of Garfit & Claypon's Boston bank.

Cures of Cunning Folk in Fen and Wold: Bed Wetting

15 DECEMBER

To cure bed wetting, it was said that girls should be taken to the grave of a boy, on which she should pass water. A boy would be taken to the grave of a girl in the same way. In other parts of the county, ground-up eggshell, given to the child in milk, allegedly sufficed.

16 DECEMBER

1834 A spirited chase took place in Heckington on this day. The village constable recruited seven men to assist in the taking of two poachers named Medlar and Burgess. Medlar was in bed when they went to his house, and made his escape out of the window wearing nothing but his shirt. He ran off, through hedges and ditches, roads and ploughed fields, without shoe or stocking. Closely pursued through seven parishes for the whole day, the hunters lost sight of him with the onset of night and were compelled to give in. The other poacher, Burgess, took shelter in a stable at Scredington under a large brewing tub; one of the pursuers, suspecting that to be the case, climbed upon it and held it down until the others arrived. Burgess was arrested.

Punishments of the Past: The Crank

17 DECEMBER

The crank was a widely adopted means of occupying prisoners in their solitary cells during the latter half of the nineteenth century. Operated by a single prisoner, the crank comprised a drum on a metal pillar, or a handle set into a wall, with a dial to register the number of times the crank handle had been turned – usually about twenty times a minute, a typical target being a total of 10,000 revolutions in eight and a half hours. If the target was not achieved in time, the prisoner was given no food until the dial registered the required total. A legacy of the crank remains today: if the prisoner found this task too easy or proved refractory, the prison warder would come and tighten the screw, making the handle harder to turn – hence the prison parlance for prison warder has, for generations, been 'the screw'.

A convict operating the crank.

18 DECEMBER   ### Strange Tales and Folklore of Lincolnshire: Three Wishes

It was once believed that, upon seeing the new moon for the first time, if you turned over the money in your pocket, turned around three times while you wished, then bowed (or curtsied) to the moon three times, your wish would come true.

It was thought that your wish would be granted upon seeing a piebald horse, if you made your wish before seeing the animal's tail.

Coal, it was said, should always be put in the Christmas stocking. Wishes were thought to come true if you took the coal, spat on it and burned it, making a wish while it burned.

1893   On this day, Henry Edward Rumbold was executed at HMP   19 DECEMBER
Lincoln by James Billington. Rumbold (37), a Grimsby smack master, was
in love with Harriet Rushby but had a fatal jealous streak. On returning
from a voyage on 17 November, he had taken her for a night out, walking
along the Cleethopes Road, visiting the Exchange public house and the
Empire Music Hall. However, Rumbold was under the misapprehension
that Harriet had been 'going with other men' and, when they returned
to where she was staying, he had pushed her upstairs. Rumbold was
then heard to say, 'If anyone comes in, I'll blow their brains out.' Then
Harriet had issued her last words: 'Don't murder me in my sins, Harry.'
Two shots had rung out and Harriet was dead.

Tried at the Lincoln Assizes, Rumbold had been found guilty and
sentenced to death. Before sentence was passed, Rumbold had admitted
to the murder and agreed it was right that he should be hanged. He had
also added that he wanted to die 'like an English hero' so he would not
be mocked by Harriet when they met in heaven. He asked permission to
have a good supply of cigars and cigarettes from the time of sentence
until his death, because he was 'a great smoker and did not want to
break down'.

1880   An alarming and destructive fire broke out at Lelham Flour Mills   20 DECEMBER
in Market Deeping. The premises were occupied by Mr and Mrs Arthur
Warwick, who were alarmed at about midnight by a strong smell of
smoke in their bedrooms and a bright light shining through the opening
of the shutters. On getting up, they found it was not their house but the
flour mills nearby that were ablaze. Assistance was obtained from the
village of West Deeping; the Deeping St James, Stamford and Burghley
House fire engines were soon on the spot but their efforts were not
successful and the mill, its contents and a large stock of corn and flour,
were all destroyed.

Tales of Lincolnshire Smuggling: Frenchies in The Wash   21 DECEMBER

Wainfleet Haven, near Gibraltar Point at the entrance to The Wash, was a
popular place for the customs sloop to lie in wait for suspected smuggling
ships. In the 1820s, while under the command of Lieutenant Butcher,
the customs sloop seized a number of vessels and cargo; in 1824, a haul
of smuggled goods on one ship included 165 tubs of Geneva, twenty-
nine bales of tobacco, two boxes of 'Segars' and a box of playing cards.
In October 1833, the Customs Officer stationed in Ingoldmells captured
a fine new smuggling vessel of 60 tons burthen. The crew were strangers
to the coast and had run the vessel ashore; she would soon have become
a wreck and most of the cargo had already been landed and carried off
into the darkness. Four Frenchmen were taken at a pub near the spot, on
suspicion of belonging to the vessel, but it was thought that they would
soon be discharged from custody 'on default of proof'. The commander of

the customs sloop at Boston, however, was warned that French smugglers put into The Wash would defend their vessels with a formidable armoury of 'cannon, swivels and muskets', and, should he give any trouble, both he and his sloop would be seized and taken to France.

22 DECEMBER 1880   During a time of popular fears over Irish rebellion and attacks by Fenians on the British mainland, this letter was published in *The Times*:

> Sir, The following incident may, perhaps, be of service at the present critical position of affairs. Last summer a farmer in Lincolnshire, was his usual custom, employed about 30 Irishmen to assist in getting in his harvest. The men at night herded together in the barn, sleeping among the straw. One night the farmer (whose name I withhold for good reasons) heard a strange noise in the barn and got up soon after midnight to see what was the matter. Imagine his surprise to find, on throwing open the barn door, all the Irishmen drilling under the command of one of their number, in perfect military fashion. The men had retired to bed long before the time when their employer discovered them at this new-found exercise.
>
> Irishmen working for farmers in Lincolnshire not unfrequently express their opinion of settling the land question by 'shooting the landlords' and hence it is fair to assume that the agitation is not altogether confined to a few straggling agitators.
>
> Yours obediently,
> OBSERVER
> Spalding, Lincolnshire.

23 DECEMBER 1847   A list of 'recent unfortunate occurrences' on the East Lincolnshire Railway was published on this day. William Archer of Authorpe had been working on the railway near Grimsby when he got the cap of his shoulder knocked off and his face badly bruised by jumping out of a ballast wagon attached to a moving engine at Holton-le-Clay.

John Blackburn had dislocated his ankle at Weelsby after falling out of a ballast wagon he was unloading. The ankle was re-set by Samuel Trought, surgeon of Louth.

Most unfortunate of all was William Spencer, a horse driver on the railway at Alford, who had fallen over a heap of ballast because the night was so dark he did not see it. A ballast wagon had then run over his right leg and crushed his left foot. Complications had developed and his leg was later amputated about 5in above the knee by Mr Odling, surgeon of Alford, who was assisted by fellow surgeons Messrs Yates and Caive. At the time the list was published, Spencer was doing well.

24 DECEMBER AD 869   An old legend tells of how the monks of Croyland (Crowland) Abbey were indulging in celebrations for the festive season that really were unbefitting for men of God. At the height of the debauchery, there was an almighty clap of thunder and the Devil appeared. He warned the monks that their time was short and that within the year their religious house would be razed and they would follow him down to the fires of hell. In AD 870, Croyland Abbey was raided by the Vikings; most of the monks were celebrating Mass and were slaughtered. The raiders then piled up the bodies and set them on fire.

The west front of Crowland Abbey.

25 DECEMBER

1816　John Maxey, a cadger of St Martin, Stamford Baron, set off with his cart to Spalding but, when near St Leonard's Priory, he was set upon by a small gang. One of them dealt him a blow across the head with a bludgeon, pulled him from the cart and rifled his pockets. They then threw him back on, beaten and bloody, and the horse plodded back to Maxey's stable of its own accord. It was thought that the gang had attempted to rob Palmer the carrier earlier that day, and had approached his cart in a suspicious manner; Palmer was all too aware of the dangers of the road and, when he had presented a pistol and asked what they wanted, his potential assailants had fled.

26 DECEMBER   **1884**   An inquest was held at Grimsby Hospital upon the body of Keziah Franklin (49) of East Street. Evidence revealed that, on Christmas night, both she and her husband had celebrated the festive season at a neighbour's house and she had returned home early, the worse for drink, at about 10 p.m. About half an hour later, cries for assistance had been heard from the Franklin residence. A fisherman lodging next door had come running and found Keziah at the top of the stairs in flames, her clothes dropping from her as they burned. The fisherman had managed to get her down and had then extinguished the flames. In the bedroom, he discovered some straw in the corner that was being used as a bed. It was in flames. This fire was also extinguished and the injured woman was conveyed to hospital, where she later died of shock. It was suggested that a candle had fallen upon the straw, setting fire to both it and Keziah. A verdict of 'accidental death' was returned.

27 DECEMBER   **1892**   An inquest was held in Gainsborough upon the body of Herbert Barlow, 'an imbecile'. He had always been a sickly child and had required constant medical treatment for most of his life. Questions were raised over the insurance for the child and the state to which he had been allowed to deteriorate. Dr Wright, who had attended Herbert, described him as thin and emaciated, and as being in a 'very filthy condition'. Herbert had also been suffering from congestion of the lungs when last examined. The doctor had warned Herbert's mother that the boy was in such a state of neglect that, should anything happen to him, he would be bound to refuse a certificate. The jury found that the child had died from natural causes, but believed his mother 'deserved censuring' for the neglect. The deputy coroner pointed out that Mrs Barlow had had a narrow escape and she must take care or she would have her other children taken away.

28 DECEMBER   **1868**   Priscilla Biggadyke (29) was executed at Lincoln Castle by Thomas Askern on this day. The case of Priscilla Biggadyke remains one of the most notorious in the annals of Lincolnshire criminal history. Richard Biggadyke (30) was a well sinker living in Mareham-le-Fen with his wife Priscilla. Although low in station, they had a tolerable standard of living and shared their house (although there was just one room for sleeping) with three children and two male lodgers – George Ironmonger and rat catcher Thomas Proctor. Richard was in the habit of leaving his wife in bed when he went to work and had, over the two months preceding, gathered suspicions over her fidelity and even began to think that the last child to be born was the result of a liaison between Proctor and his wife.

TRIAL AND EXECUTION

PRISCILLA BIGGADIKE,

For the wilful Murder of her Husband on the 1st of October, 1868, who was tried before the Right Hon. Sir John Barnard BYLES, Knight, on Friday Dec. 11th.

She was Executed in private at the South End of the County Hall, Lincoln Castle, MONDAY morning, DECEMBER 28th, 1868.

THE TRIAL.

THE STICKNEY MURDER.

PRISCILLA BIGGADIKE, widow, 29, was charged with the wilful murder of Richard Biggadike, her husband, at Stickney, on the 1st of October, 1868.

Mr. Bristowe and Mr. Horace Smith appeared on behalf of the prosecution; Mr. Lawrence defended the prisoner.

Mr. Bristowe, at considerable length, detailed to the jury all the principal facts of the case, and the circumstances under which the murder was committed revealed a depth of moral depravity and social degradation we could fain hope has no parallel elsewhere in the county of Lincoln. The following witnesses were examined :—

James Turner said he knew the deceased and he always appeared to enjoy excellent health.

George Ironmonger said : I lodged in the house with deceased. Mrs. Biggadike, Proctor, and I had tea together before deceased came home on Wednesday evening, Sept. 30th. We had two "short cakes," which were made by Mrs. B., who did all the cooking. I went out after tea, and when I returned deceased was just finishing his tea, and seemed quite well. He got up a few minutes after and went to the privy, and I heard him retching, and very sick. After he had returned he went again, and then he said, "I am very bad; I can't live long this how; send for the doctor." I fetched the doctor immediately. Deceased died at six next morning. I was upstairs once during the night.

Peter Maxwell, surgeon, deposed : I was called to deceased at seven o'clock on Wednesday evening, Sept 30. I found him in great pain in bed, sick, and violently purged. He had all the symptoms of poisoning by some irritant poison. I sent him suitable medicines, and saw him again at eleven o'clock, when he was collapsed and rapidly getting worse. I heard he died early next morning. On the 2nd October I made a post-mortem examination of the body. The head and chest were perfectly free from disease. I removed the viscera and contents of the stomach, placed them in jars &c., duly sealed, and handed over to to Supt. Wright I believe deceased died from the effects of poison.

Supt. Wright, of Spilsby, deposed : On the 2nd October I received one jar and three bottles, sealed and secured by Mr. Maxwell. On the 6th I delivered them to Dr. Taylor, Guy's Hospital. I apprehended the prisoner, and then charged her with wilfully murdering her own husband. I cautioned her very strongly not to criminate herself. She said "'tis hard work I should bear all the blame alone."

Dr. Alfred Swaine Taylor stated that he was a Fellow of the College of Physicians, and Professor of Medical Jurisprudence at Guy's Hospital. On Tuesday the 6th of Oct. he received certain jars from Supt. Wright, containing the contents of the stomach of Rd. Biggadike. Dr. Taylor's evidence was very lengthy, full of the usual scientific details, and showed that he had not the slightest doubt that the deceased had died through the administration of arsenic, which was the only conclusion he could draw from the results of his analysis.

Mary Ann Clarke said : I am a widow residing at Stickney, and close to Biggadike's. On the 30th I heard a noise in their house as of many people talking, and went to see what was the matter. Proctor sat against the door, and he said, "Dick's very bad since he got his tea." A short time after the prisoner came to my house with a piece of cake in her hand, and she said, "the doctor says I've put something into the cake which I ought not to have done, but I hav'nt. I heard deceased in his agony say, "the Lord have mercy upon me." He died while I was there.

Jane Ironmonger said : I saw deceased in bed very sick and bad. I asked the prisoner if she had sent for his brother, and she said, "No, it does not matter, for they have not been on very good terms lately." I fetched his brother. We found the prisoner and two lodgers in the lower room. I was there when he died. On one occasion I heard the prisoner say she hoped her husband might be brought home dead, and another time she said she wished he might be brought home stiff. She then asked me how the murderers Garniers (of Marchiant-le-Fen) got on about their poisoning case. She said they searched the meal and sago.

Thomas Proctor said : On the 30th of September last I lodged at Biggadike's. On that day I went fishing with George Ironmonger, a fellow lodger. We came home together to tea, and afterwards went fishing again. Ironmonger went first, leaving Mrs. Biggadike, and the child in the house. I never put any white powder in a tea cup, neither on that occasion or any other I had no white powder or poison in my possession. I am a rat-catcher, and keep ferrets, but never keep any poison. When we came home from fishing, Mrs. Biggadike was in the house and her husband. He was taken very ill, and continued so all night. I remained with him until he died. The prisoner prepared our food.

The jury, after a consultation of only a few minutes, returned a verdict of GUILTY, accompanied by a recommendation to mercy, but upon the Judge asking upon what grounds, the foreman of the jury seemed perplexed, and again consulted with his fellows for a short time, and then said that the only ground for such recommendation was that the evidence was entirely circumstantial.

His Lordship then put on the black cap, and amidst the most solemn silence passed the sentence of death upon the unhappy woman. In addressing her his Lordship said : Priscilla Biggadike, although the evidence against you is only circumstantial, yet more satisfactory and conclusive evidence I never heard in my life. You must now prepare for your impending fate, by attending to the religious instruction you will receive, to which, if you had given heed before, you would never have stood in your present unhappy position The sentence of the court is that you be taken to the place from whence you came, and thence to the place of execution, there to be hanged by the neck till you and may the Lord have mercy upon your soul to be buried within the precincts of the pri then walked firmly away from the lasted seven hours.

A broadside recounting the trial of Priscilla Biggadyke, sold at her execution.

On 30 September, Richard had sat down to a meal of mutton followed by shortcake made by Priscilla. Within ten minutes, he was retching and had excruciating pain in his stomach; he had died in agony the following morning. Analysis of his stomach by Professor Taylor revealed a large quantity of arsenic. When suspicion fell upon Priscilla, who had made comments to the effect that she wished her husband dead, she immediately tried to deflect them onto Proctor, whom she said had put white powder into a teacup and also into the medicine ordered for her husband. Proctor was taken into custody. The confused statements of Priscilla did not help her and she was placed in the House of Correction. Soon, both Proctor and Biggadyke were brought before the Assizes. The case against Proctor had not held up and he was soon acquitted; the main thrust of the prosecution had then turned upon Priscilla. She was found guilty of the murder on what was essentially circumstantial evidence and was sentenced to death. Despite her family and the prison chaplain imploring her to confess and clear her mind, Priscilla protested her innocence to the gallows where, after she was prepared by the executioner, her last words before the traps fell were, 'Oh! You won't hang me!' Once she had dropped, it was noted that 'she appeared to suffer a good deal before her strong vital powers succumbed'. The twist in this tale came in 1882. Thomas Proctor, lying on his deathbed, confessed that he had indeed committed the murder. (*See also* 26 May)

29 DECEMBER **1886** Charles Ludlow (13) and William Quincy were skating on a large brick pit in Quadring Fen when the ice gave way and both boys tragically drowned. In 1892, an inquest was held upon the body of Robert Ranby (70), who lived at North Forty Foot Bank. Ranby had been found dead on the ice of the dyke the previous day. Medical evidence showed that Ranby had suffered from concussion of the brain and exposure. A verdict was returned accordingly.

30 DECEMBER **1937** On this day, Fredrick Nodder was executed at HMP Lincoln. Nodder (45) was a motor engineer of Hatton Heath, near Retford, Nottingham. He had been found guilty of murdering Mona Tinsley (10), whose body was found in the River Idle near Bawtry on 6 June, five months after she had disappeared. She had been strangled. After the guilty verdict was returned at his trial, when asked if he had anything to say, Nodder had replied, 'I shall go out of this court with a clear conscience.' The judge commented, 'Justice has slowly but surely overtaken you.' With the death sentence passed upon him, Nodder was taken down, smiling to himself.

31 DECEMBER **1852** On this day, an inquest was held at the Lock Tavern, Louth, upon the body of William Rhodes (24), mate of the sloop *Queen of Louth and Grimsby*, who was found drowned in the river near to his vessel. From the

The tragic end of
William Rhodes.

evidence presented, it appeared that Rhodes had been drinking at the
house of his fiancée's father. He had returned to his vessel worse for
drink and had gone to the bows to defecate; straining too hard, he
had fallen overboard in the process and drowned. The jury returned a
verdict accordingly.

BIBLIOGRAPHY

Books

Anderson, C.L., *Convicts of Lincolnshire* (Lincoln, 1988)

Andrews, William, *Bygone Lincolnshire* (London, 1891)

Anon., *The Wonderful Discoverie of the Witchcrafts of Margaret and Phillip Flower* (London 1619, reprinted Leicester 1970)

Arthur, Jane, ed., *Medicine in Wisbech and the Fens* (Wisbech, 1985)

Butler, Ivan, *Murderers' England* (London, 1973)

Chambers, Robert, *The Book of Days* (London, 1869)

Dring, W.E., *The Fenland Story* (Cambridge, 1967)

Field, Naomi and White, Andrew, *A Prospect of Lincolnshire* (Lincoln, 1984)

Gray, Adrian, *Crime and Criminals in Victorian Lincolnshire* (Stamford, 1993)

Gray, Adrian, *Lincolnshire Tales of Mystery and Murder* (Newbury, 2004)

Harper, Charles, *Half-hours with the Highwaymen* (London, 1908)

Harries, John, *The Ghost Hunter's Road Book* (London, 1974)

Heanley, Robert, *Folklore of the Lincolnshire Marsh* (1902, reprinted Burgh le Marsh 2008)

Hippisley Coxe, A.D., *Haunted Britain* (London, 1973)

Hissey, James John, *Over Fen and Wold* (London, 1898)

Hone, William, *The Every-Day Book and Table Book* (London, 1826)

Hope Robbins, Rossell, *The Encyclopaedia of Witchcraft and Demonology* (Feltham, 1959)

Howat, Polly, *Ghosts & Legends of Lincolnshire and the Fen Country* (Newbury, 1992)

Jackson, William, *The New and Complete Newgate Calendar; or Malefactor's Universal Register* vols I-VI (London, 1795-1807)

Ketteringham, John R., *A Lincolnshire Hotchpotch* (Revised Edition, Lincoln, 1990)

Ketteringham, John R., *A Second Lincolnshire Hotchpotch* (Revised Edition, Lincoln, 1990)

Kirby, R.S., *Kirby's Wonderful and Scientific Museum* (London, 1820)

Knapp, Andrew and Baldwin, William, *The Newgate Calendar* (London, 1824)

Lane, Brian, *The Murder Club Guide to The Midlands* (London, 1988)

Lincolnshire Federations of Women's Institutes, *The Lincolnshire Village Book* (Newbury, 1990)

Marlowe, Christopher, *The Fen Country* (London, 1926)

Mee, Arthur, *Lincolnshire* (King's England Series, Revised Edition, London, 1970)

Pelham, Camden, *The Chronicles of Crime or the New Newgate Calendar* (London, 1886)

Rudkin, Ethel H., *Lincolnshire Lore* (Gainsborough 1936, reprinted Burgh le Marsh 2003)

Summers, Montague, *Geography of Witchcraft* (London, 1927)

Timpson, John, *Timpson's England* (Norwich, 1997)

Wade, Stephen, *Hanged at Lincoln* (Stroud, 2009)

Wedlake Brayley, Edward, *The Beauties of England and Wales* (London, 1808)

Wentworth Day, James, *Here are Ghosts & Witches* (London, 1954)

Wentworth Day, James, *In Search of Ghosts* (London, 1969)

Wood, G. Bernard, *Smugglers' Britain* (London, 1966)

Newspapers, Periodicals and Directories

Boston Standard
Daily Express
Daily Mirror
Daily News
Fenland Notes & Queries
Grantham Journal
Hull & Lincolnshire Times
Hull Packet & East Riding Times
Illustrated London News
Illustrated Police News
Lincolnshire, Boston & Spalding Free Press
Lincolnshire Echo
Lincolnshire Notes & Queries
Spalding Guardian
Stamford Mercury
Strand Magazine
The Tablet
The Times
Kelly's Directory of Lincolnshire, 1876
Pigot's Directory of Lincolnshire, 1835 and 1841

APPENDIX

Executions Conducted at Lincoln Castle 1817 – 1877

Executed upon the roof of Cobb Hall

Date of Execution	Name of Condemned	Offence for which they hanged
15 March 1817	Elizabeth Whiting	Murder of her baby by poisoning
26 July 1817	Elizabeth Warriner	Murder of her stepson John Warriner
15 August 1817	William Longland	Burglary at Grantham
27 March 1818	Richard Randall	Highway robbery at Holbeach
27 March 1818	John Tubbs	Highway robbery at Holbeach
27 March 1818	Thomas Morris	Arson at Anwick
27 March 1818	Thomas Evison	Arson at Anwick
19 March 1819	John Louth	Housebreaking at Pinchbeck
16 August 1819	Richard Johnson	Horse stealing
17 March 1820	William Fox	Rape at Tathwell
23 March 1821	David Booth	Housebreaking at Whaplode
23 March 1821	John Parrish	Housebreaking at Whaplode
9 August 1821	James Cawthorne	Murder of Mary Cawthorne, his wife
22 March 1822	John Rogers	Highway robbery
2 August 1822	Joseph Burkitt	Highway robbery
21 March 1823	Benjamin Candler	Sodomy
21 March 1823	William Arden	Sodomy
21 March 1823	John Doughty	Sodomy
15 March 1824	John Smith	Murder of Sarah Arrowsmith at Alford
20 August 1824	James Wetherill	Murder of William Berridge at Brigg
23 March 1827	William Udale	Stealing sheep at Long Sutton
27 March 1829	Thomas Lister	Burglary at Halstead Hall
27 March 1829	George Wingfield	Highway robbery near Sleaford
19 March 1830	Thomas Strong	Burglary at Halstead Hall
19 March 1830	Timothy Brammer	Burglary at Halstead Hall
19 March 1830	John Clarke	Sheep stealing at Freiston
12 March 1831	Michael Lundy	Murder of Thomas Sewards, his father-in-law
18 March 1831	John Greenwood	Housebreaking at Theddlethorpe All Saints

22 July 1831	William Hall	Murder of Edward Button at Grimsby
29 July 1831	Richard Cooling	Arson at Lusby
29 July 1831	Thomas Motley	Arson at Lusby
18 March 1833	William Taylor	Murder of William Burbank at Heckington
27 March 1833	William Stephenson	Highway robbery near Burgh le Marsh
26 July 1833	Thomas Knapton	Rape at Gainsborough
17 March 1843	Thomas Johnson	Murder of the Evinson sisters
2 August 1844	Eliza Joyce	Murder of her son William by poisoning
27 July 1849	John Ward	Matricide at Thorpe
5 August 1859	Henry Carey	Murder of William Stevenson at Sibsey
5 August 1859	William Pickett	Murder of William Stevenson at Sibsey

Executions within the walls of Lincoln Castle after the Capital Punishment Act of 1868

28 December 1868	Priscilla Biggadyke	Murder of Richard Biggadyke, her husband
1 April 1872	William Horry	Murder of Jane Horry, his wife at Boston
9 August 1875	Peter Blanchard	Murder of Louise Hodgson at Louth
26 March 1877	William Clarke	Murder of gamekeeper Henry Walker

The Lucy Tower burial ground, for those who died or were executed at Lincoln Castle between 1824 and 1877.

Other titles published by The History Press

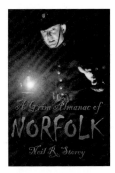

A Grim Almanac of Norfolk

NEIL R. STOREY

This almanac explores dreadful deeds, macabre deaths, strange occurrences and grim tales from the shadier side of Norfolk's past. Jostling for position in this cornucopia of the criminal and curious are diverse tales of highwaymen, smugglers, murderers, bodysnatchers, duellists, footpads, poachers, rioters and rebels. This sordid cast of characters is deservedly accompanied by accounts of lock-ups, prisons and punishments, as well as a liberal smattering of bizarre funerals, disasters and peculiar medicine.

978 0 7524 5680 5

Murder & Crime Lincoln

DOUGLAS WYNN

The historic city of Lincoln has a history going back to the Romans and a catalogue of crimes to match. John Haigh, the 'Acid Bath Murderer', was born in nearby Stamford and was imprisoned in Lincoln – where he experimented on small animals to perfect his acid-bath techniques. The city also has its share of women who drowned unwanted babies in the nearby River Witham, and husbands who beat their wives to death. Combining meticulous research with evocative photography, the author provides a feast of crime to haunt the imagination.

978 0 7524 5921 9

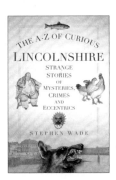

The A-Z of Curious Lincolnshire

STEPHEN WADE

Filled with hilarious and surprising examples of folklore, eccentrics, and historical and literary events, all taken from Lincolnshire's tumultuous history, the reader will meet forgers, poets, aristocrats, politicians and some less likely residents of the county, including Spring Heel'd Jack and the appearance of an angel in Gainsborough. This is the county that brought us Lord Tennyson (whose brother was treated at an experimental asylum in the area), John Wesley, and notorious hangman William Marwood; here too were found the Dam Busters, the first tanks and the fishing fleets of Grimsby.

978 0 7524 6027 7

Murder & Crime Boston

DOUGLAS WYNN

Stabbings, shootings, poisonings and stranglings have all made it into the pages of Boston's history. Young and old, husbands and wives, parents and children, and even complete strangers fell victim to murderous attacks. The motives for such atrocious crimes ranged from overwhelming jealousy and blinding rage to calculated greed and petty disputes. These fourteen tales from the late nineteenth and early twentieth centuries will fascinate everyone wanting to know more about Boston's dark history.

978 0 7524 5544 0

Visit our website and discover thousands of other History Press books.
www.thehistorypress.co.uk